Valiant Companions

Helen Keller and Her "Miracle Worker"

By Helen Elmira Waite

Cover Design by Wayne Blickenstaff

SCHOLASTIC BOOK SERVICES

Published by Scholastic Book Services, a division
of Scholastic Magazines, Inc., New York, N.Y.

The author wishes to thank Doubleday and Co., Inc. for permission to reprint excerpts from THE STORY OF MY LIFE by Helen Keller, copyright 1903, 1931 by Helen Keller; MIDSTREAM by Helen Keller; HELEN KELLER'S JOURNAL by Helen Keller, and ANNE SULLIVAN MACY by Nella Braddy, copyright 1933 by Nella Braddy.

3rd printing...............................December 1967

Printed in the U.S.A.

AUTHOR'S NOTE

All persons, places and incidents mentioned in this book are authentic, and the conversations are based upon the writings of Helen Keller, Anne Sullivan Macy and other firsthand sources.

All reports and letters dealing with Mr. Gilman's attempt to separate Annie Sullivan from her pupil were preserved by Dr. Alexander Graham Bell and are on file in the Bell Room of the National Geographic Society, Washington, D.C.

The author extends her grateful thanks to Miss Helen Keller for her gracious permission to write this biography; to Mr. Nelson Coon, Librarian of the Perkins School for the Blind, and his assistant, Miss Florence J. Worth, for their cordial hospitality and generous assistance; to Mr. Daniel J. Burns, Head of the Deaf-Blind Department, and his staff, for the opportunity to see the present-day teaching methods for deaf-blind children; to Miss Gayle Sabonatis, for a personal glimpse into the daily life of a deaf-blind girl; and, last but by no means least, to Miss Helen M. Vreeland for her invaluable assistance during our stay at the Perkins School.

For

My Own Valiant Companion

Helen M. Vreeland

CONTENTS

CHAPTER · 1

The Triumphant Day

"Now just one more thing, and you'll be ready." Mrs. Hopkins pushed the last ringlet of hair gently into place and stood back to survey her handiwork, first speculatively, and then with approval. "Mr. Anagnos is right. You do look like Miss Frances Folsom."

Stealing a quick look in the mirror over Mrs. Hopkins' bureau, Annie had a quick shiver of delight. It still seemed miraculous to think that she, who had been practically blind the first sixteen years of her life, could actually see herself in a mirror! Yes, she could see for herself that she did resemble Frances Folsom, the girl who was President Cleveland's

1

bride! Mrs. Hopkins had piled the very dark hair high on her head, and then made ringlets over her forehead with her own curling iron, and in her fine muslin dress with its elbow sleeves and three ruffles edged with lace Annie could have been taken for a bride herself. She wondered if the Bride of the White House could have been more excited than Annie Sullivan was at this moment.

"Now," Mrs. Hopkins said again, and turned toward a mysterious box on the bed. Annie gasped, for out of a bed of tissue paper appeared a wide sash of gleaming pink satin. The older woman's fingers caressed it before she looked at Annie. "It was Florence's," she said quietly. "She wore it at her graduation. I want you to have it today."

It was like an accolade, for Annie knew how Mrs. Hopkins cherished all of the possessions of the daughter whose life had been so brief.

"And now I have another girl who's graduating." Mrs. Hopkins gave the sash a final pat, and nodded approval. "You'll do. Time to go now. Mr. Anagnos wouldn't be pleased if the valedictorian is late."

The feeling of incredulity which had been rising in Annie all day strengthened when they reached Tremont Temple where the commencements of the Perkins Institution and Massachusetts School for the Blind were held. Could she—Annie Sullivan—actually be the valedictorian of this graduating class of 1886? At the steps of the platform her favorite teacher, Miss Mary Moore, smiled at her as she pinned a corsage of pink roses at her belt. Somehow the touch of their petals made her feel faint. Then Mr. Anagnos, Director of Perkins, had taken her hand to lead her to her seat; he was murmuring words of encouragement which blurred in her ears. She was shivering again, and not from joy this time.

The audience. How could she ever face it? So many people. And such famous ones, like Mrs. Julia Ward Howe, the author of "Battle Hymn of the Republic," Mrs. Livermore, an ardent advocate of women's rights, and the Governor of Massachusetts. She sat through the music and the speeches, feeling more and more frozen, her throat tightening by the minute, and then suddenly it was her turn. The Governor looked in her direction with a gracious gesture and announced: "The valedictory—by Miss Annie Mansfield Sullivan!"

Annie managed to rise, but her knees were trembling so that she knew they would never support her. She hesitated so long that the Governor spoke her name again. And then she summoned all her courage to walk toward the center of the platform. The kindly man led the polite applause, and after a somewhat faint "Ladies and gentlemen—" Annie was amazed and relieved to hear her voice lifting clearly and easily in the little speech she had written and rehearsed so often. The world was slipping back into focus, and she could meet the interested, friendly gaze of the audience with confidence. She had a quick thrill of triumph. And then she had finished and was bowing to another round of applause, not merely polite this time, but spontaneous and exciting.

After the program her impressions seemed hurried and confused. She knew Dr. Samuel Eliot, one of Perkins' trustees, praised her speech, and Mr. Anagnos was alternately beaming and blowing his nose. "You were a credit to Perkins, my dear Annie, a great credit. And when I remember how you came to us six years ago—"

Miss Moore had no time for anything but a swift kiss, and Mrs. Hopkins couldn't get close enough even for that. But her classmates and the other Perkins pupils crowded around with congratulations, eager to "see" her. With the understanding born of her own blindness, Annie gave them all ample time to let their delicately exploring fingers travel over her dress and her fashionable hairdo, while she laughingly answered their comments and praise. Even Laura Bridgman, the famous deaf, mute, and blind member of the Institution was there, as she always was on important occasions at Perkins.

And then it really was over, and she was back in her own little room at school. She closed the door softly. The other girls were still reliving the excitement of commencement, but she had to be alone for her final taste of the wonder and beauty of this incredible day.

Very slowly she unpinned the pink roses and placed them in a glass of water. Reluctantly she unfastened the sash and smoothed it on the bed with loving fingers, wondering if she would ever wear it again. But the dress was certainly her own. How good Mrs. Hopkins, busy as she was with her duties as matron of Annie's cottage, had been to make it for her. She sat on the edge of her bed, touching the tiny buttons as though they were real pearls, and loving the ruffles and lace.

It did require real will power to remove the white slippers—Annie Sullivan owning white slippers! Her eyes darkened suddenly. She was remembering the Annie Sullivan who had come to Perkins six years ago. That Annie Sullivan had been fourteen, practically blind. She had been the most unkempt, untaught, unmanageable, the shabbiest specimen of a girl Perkins had ever received. The only clothing she had had to her name had been two coarse chemises and two calico dresses.

"Annie!" the girls were calling her eagerly. "An-nie!"

Annie pretended not to hear. This was a moment she could not share.

Her memories went on. Her first day at Perkins had been a bitter one. The teacher she encountered first of all asked her name and age. She could give that, but when the teacher asked her to spell a word, she could only mumble, "I can't. I can't spell anything!"

"Fourteen years old and can't spell!" the teacher had never met up with such a condition. She said

5

so, and Annie had sensed her scorn. But worse was to come. The blind girls crowded around the newcomer, felt for her belongings, and then questioned in astonishment:

"Where are your clothes and the rest of your things?"

Annie had been obliged to shake her head and acknowledge ashamedly that she had none. The girls in the cottage to which she had been assigned had never heard of a girl who didn't possess a coat, hat, extra shoes—not even a toothbrush. They said so, and they laughed. And Annie had hated all of them.

"Why didn't your mother make you some things?"

"My mother's dead," Annie had said shortly, "and so's my little brother. And that's all."

Well, it was all the family she would acknowledge. She did have a father, and a sister; but nothing would have dragged the fact out of her that when her mother had died four years before, her shiftless, unreliable father had abandoned his family. An aunt had taken her lovable baby sister, but none of the relatives wanted to be saddled with a nearly blind girl and a small boy with a tubercular hip, so they had been shunted off to the Tewksbury Almshouse, one of the most miserable institutions of its kind in the country. The conditions there had killed Jimmie within two months, but Annie had spent four wretched years there until the State

Board of Charities had sent Frank B. Sanborn to investigate.

Annie remembered how she had run through the wards the day of his inspection, crying, "Mr. Sanborn! Mr. Sanborn!" and when a man's voice answered her, she burst out desperately, "I can't see very well and I want to go to school!"

And so she escaped Tewksbury. When she left, one old woman, who had been genuinely kind to her, cautioned, "Don't never tell nobody you came from the poorhouse," and Annie had promised with vehemence, "I won't!"

The teachers and officials knew, of course, but Annie would sooner have died than reveal it to the pupils.

So scantily had she been provided for that the matron of her cottage had to borrow a nightgown for her that first night, and poor, fiercely proud, and friend-hungry Annie had cried herself to sleep that night—yes, and for many nights.

When she stepped into Perkins it was almost as though she had stepped upon another planet. Not only did she have to begin her education with the first grade, but she had to learn to live a life she had never known existed. Always the Sullivans had been desperately poor, her mother had always been ill, and life at Tewksbury had been grim. Here at Perkins her schoolmates were fortunate children, despite their blindness; they were children of doctors, merchants, lawyers, prosperous farmers. The girls in Annie's cottage were happy, sheltered girls, and none of Annie's experiences had taught her how to lead a happy, sheltered life.

No wonder she had been confused, difficult, and defiant. If she had been an easily defeated person her first year at Perkins would certainly have crushed her, but Annie Sullivan would never be a person to surrender. She had come to Perkins to learn, and learn she did, swiftly, forging ahead to take her place with classmates of her own age. But more than that, she learned at Perkins to seek beauty, and truth, and justice.

Perkins had been good to her. Most of her teachers had been kind. They'd clothed her, given her special lessons, stood between her and a return to Tewksbury, when her defiance had almost stretched the authorities' patience to the breaking point; had seen that she had free tickets to lectures and concerts. But the thing that she would always be passionately grateful for was that someone had suggested there might be hope for her eyes, and had arranged to have her taken to the Eye Clinic on one of the free days. After that there were two operations, one when she was fifteen, the second exactly a year later, and when they were over Annie could see. Oh, not perfectly—Dr. Bradford had warned her she would never do that, and she must always avoid over-using or straining her eyes, but she could see. She could learn to read print, see the bricks in a building across the river, and the day she discovered that she actually could thread a needle without using her tongue, she almost died of sheer joy.

She had remained at Perkins after her sight was restored because there really was no other place for her to go. She had earned her way by helping with the teaching and the care of the smaller children, but now—what was she to do now? She knew only too well that thought had been troubling her friends for the past several weeks. Would she—would she have to return to Tewksbury after all? The thought made her throat tighten with fear.

Resolutely she stood up and began putting her dainty things away. The supper bell was ringing. Annie summoned all her courage. She would go down and be as gay and excited as any girl at the cottage, and for tonight no one should guess that she wasn't the happiest girl in the city of Boston.

Perhaps one person did know. One wouldn't have suspected the prim-appearing, typically New England widow, Mrs. Hopkins, of being a kindred spirit to restless, temper-tossed Annie Sullivan, but as long as Mrs. Hopkins lived there would be a special bond of understanding between them. Now, as the girl descended the stairs, the matron paused in her bustling about the dining room to smile proudly at Annie.

"You did beautifully, dear," she told her, "just as I knew you would."

"It took the courage of a thousand Irish chieftains," Annie confessed ruefully, "I was so ashamed when the Governor had to call my name a second time."

From the end of the table where she was deftly seating her small charges, Miss Moore smiled at her. "We were all proud of you, Annie!" Coming from Mary Moore the words had special meaning, and Annie was doubly grateful. Mary Moore had been the teacher who had given special time and patience to teaching and taming the willful, ignorant, capricious child Annie had been. Sometimes Annie suspected that Miss Moore knew how to "get her under her thumb" better than anyone else, but she adored her for all that.

"Sit here by me, Annie!" "No, I want her with me tonight!" "Oh, Annie, please come sit by us!" The younger girls chorused eagerly, and anxious little hands reached out imploringly, but Annie gently evaded them all.

"I'm going to sit by Laura, tonight," she announced, and went to take her place beside a stiffly erect, silent woman, whose strangely fixed expression made her a rather weird figure in the midst of this lively group. At the touch of Annie's hand, however, her face lighted instantly, reminding those who could see her of sunlight on rippling waters. She made a series of butterfly-quick gestures in the air, and Annie replied with the same finger-talk in Laura's hand, because for deaf, mute, and blind

Laura Bridgman the only means of communication with others was this finger alphabet used by the deaf. All the teachers, matrons, and pupils could use it, for Perkins had been Laura's home since she was seven. Somehow Annie had acquired a special skill with it, and she was one of Laura's favorites.

Now, seated beside her at supper, Laura began spelling out eager, staccato questions, and Annie answered with flying fingers, describing the goings-on around the table between bites, and promising to go to Laura's own room later to tell her about Commencement.

Commencement had really been a success. The Boston papers even said very flattering things about the valedictorian, which made delightful reading, but did not answer the question that kept nagging at the valedictorian's mind: What was she to do now—what could a girl do, anyway, who would go through life with a painful eye condition and defective sight?

No one had produced a satisfactory solution by the time Perkins closed for the summer, and although Annie smiled and held her head high with an Irish jauntiness, her worry had become a fear that was always lurking in the background of her consciousness and sometimes darted out to give an unexpected jab.

"You are coming to Brewster with me as usual, of course," Mrs. Hopkins had informed her decisively, "and if anything promising turns up, you can be notified in Brewster just as easily as if you were in Boston."

Mr. Anagnos agreed. "She is right, my dear Annie. Quite right. And all the teachers as well as myself have you in mind. We'll let you know immediately, never fear." He patted her hand reassuringly. "Now go and enjoy your summer, my dear."

Annie's lips felt stiff as she thanked him, and her smile was difficult to manage.

She accepted Mrs. Hopkins' invitation gratefully, but she realized this was only a stopgap, and she faced the fact soberly, and when the door of the cottage which that good lady headed as matron (there were several cottages on the Perkins' grounds), snapped shut after them, it had the sound of doom to Annie's ears.

The Perkins Institution and Massachusetts School for the Blind was the only place she could call "home." Was its door closing upon her forever?

CHAPTER · 2

Challenge From Alabama

THERE WAS SOMETHING about the Cape Cod village of Brewster which restored Annie's natural resiliency of spirit, exactly as Mrs. Hopkins had expected it would. Sophia Hopkins knew and understood the girl better than Annie ever dreamed, and perhaps she never did realize how deeply the matron had influenced her.

This Sophia Hopkins had come to Perkins because she desperately wanted to give herself to somebody or some cause that really needed her. Her sea-captain husband had met his death on a voyage years before, and her beloved only daughter had died recently. Her sturdily independent mother was

13

much happier left to herself, and Sophia was not a person to live an empty life. She had noticed some blind boys playing on the beach one day, and the thought flashed upon her: Now there's the work for me! When she applied she was promptly engaged to be matron of the cottage where Annie had been living for three years.

Annie had been making progress in her studies, but she was still ragged emotionally, unloved and unloving. Mrs. Hopkins was good to all her girls, which could be the reason several of them turned out to be really outstanding people. Little Lydia Hayes, for example, became the head of the New Jersey Commission for the Blind. It was evident to Mrs. Hopkins that in Annie Sullivan she found a person who really needed her, and she promptly took the girl under her wing, loving her, and gentling her regardless of Annie's resistance and waywardness. Some instinct taught the older woman that all Annie's exhibitions and dark moods were a barrier she was holding up to protect a bewildered, resentful, troubled girl's soul against fresh hurts, and that underneath it all a finely molded, sensitive nature was waiting to be discovered. Just then Annie's future was a question mark. She might be embittered and warped by her Tewksbury experiences and her early struggles at Perkins—or just because of them she might emerge with a greater understanding for everyone handicapped or hurt.

"She has it in her to do wonderful things, some

day," Mrs. Hopkins had said, defending her to a teacher who had been greatly provoked by Annie's saucy behavior one Exhibition Day. Exhibition Days were a policy at Perkins, days when the school was thrown open to visitors who were free to wander about the different classrooms, and see the school in action. Annie usually was called upon to recite, for her quick, intelligent answers showed the Perkins methods to advantage, but on this particular day when the teacher asked, "What was the best thing King John ever did?" Annie had been inspired to answer impishly, "I haven't decided," and stubbornly refused to add another word. Perhaps it was small wonder the teacher was skeptical, but Mrs. Hopkins was firm in her own conviction.

"She has it in her to do some wonderful things," she repeated, "and a very great capacity for loving if we can ever get at her heart."

But rebellious and capricious though she was, Annie would never, in all her life, be proof against genuine kindness and sympathy, and Mrs. Hopkins had those in abundance. Annie had never been loved before, and she found it rather strange—but she rejoiced in it, and began experimenting with practicing it herself. She took the smaller blind girls on walks, or to church on Sundays, helped them with their lessons, comforted the homesick, lonely ones. Annie was well acquainted with loneliness. Perhaps it was about this time that she began her friendly companionship with Laura Bridgman.

When Perkins closed for the summer of 1884, Mrs. Hopkins for the first time invited Annie to spend the vacation in her and her mother's home in Brewster. Annie never forgot the thrill of incredulous joy that swept over her. Heretofore she had been sent where she might work for her keep during the summer, but an actual invitation—to be really wanted.

And Brewster. She fell in love with the place within the first fortnight. The clean sweep of sky; the snug, attractive houses, so different from Boston's square, stolid-looking buildings; the narrow, meandering, sandy roads; the fragrant, open fields; the stretches of golden beach, broken by little islands of stiff beach grass—all these combined to make it the first place Annie had ever seen that satisfied her passionate hunger for beauty.

And the people—they answered some craving in her, too, with their firm self-reliance, vigorous outlook, and unexpected twists of humor. She had never lived among completely normal people before, people who accepted her as a matter of course, and she rejoiced in every day she spent in Brewster.

The Crocker house added to her delight. Like her husband, Mrs. Hopkins' father had been a sea captain, and the house was brimming with trophies from his voyages, especially the parlor. Annie never would list dusting among her favorite occupations, but she was always more than ready to "rid up" the parlor. Anything that took her into the Crocker parlor would have its compensations.

Even Annie felt a little awed whenever she entered this room. First she would steal carefully across the precious carpet (there were no carpets or rugs at Perkins) and open a few slats of the window blinds, and then go straight to the whatnot that held her favorite treasures: Chinese figures, dainty music boxes, smooth ivory elephants. She was entranced by them all. Elsewhere in the room were a set of blue china brought from Holland with pictures of a harbor and town on the various pieces, exquisite silver goblets from Portugal, and a magnificent, prism-hung lamp. But Annie's favorites stood on the mantel—two dainty china dolls bearing baskets of fruit and flowers. Another girl might have needed Aunt Crocker's admonition against careless or unnecessary handling, but to Annie Sullivan sight was still such a miracle that just to stand and feast her eyes upon the treasure trove was sufficient joy, and when she did dust them it was with the tender touch of the blind child she had been.

But even in Brewster Annie had walked with a wayward spirit. Sometime after their arrival Mrs. Hopkins had pointed out a certain narrow path and informed Annie that it led "to a filthy cave where a crazy old hermit lived." That would have been warning enough to have kept any of the docile, properly brought up girls at Perkins at a very safe distance, but docility and caution had never been Annie's strong points. "Bedeviled by curiosity," she followed the path as soon as possible through the tall, tickling grass and found that the path opened at last upon a wide plateau of smooth beach. There was an odd-looking shack, and an old man, very clean, who reminded her of Rip Van Winkle.

"Hello," said Annie, in her most casual voice.

Roused from a nap, the hermit wasn't exactly cordial on that occasion. He scowled at her, telling her he didn't need visitors—didn't like company, especially "wimmin." But perhaps he sensed her simple, straightforward fearlessness, for he grunted, and finally invited her to "set." He looked at her curiously from under bushy, grizzled brows.

"Ain't ye afraid of me?"

Annie shook her head. "No, not now. I was at first. But you're not crazy."

"Well, now, thank ye!" The old man bowed. "Don't know how ye know, but I'm not. You've got more sense'n most. Don't come from Brewster, do ye?"

Annie admitted that she didn't, and the hermit chuckled in satisfaction. " 'Course ye don't! Got too much sense!"

He was a picturesque person in his faded blue overalls, with his crinkling blue eyes and snowy beard, and with his brown feet bare. Annie's frank remark seemed to have disarmed him for when she rose to go he sociably invited her to "come agin."

She did. Somehow she convinced Mrs. Hopkins that while undoubtedly he was a hermit and might be queer, crazy he was not.

So, despite Aunt Crocker's outspoken disapproval, Annie was allowed to visit the Hermit of Brewster not only once, but several times that summer and the next. They established a friendship Annie remembered all her life—the young girl and the old man, who probably was lonelier than he would admit. He told her stories of his adventurous days at sea, though he always evaded the question of his name. Annie took to calling him "Captain Dad," and he called her "Daughter" in return. He did her the honor of taking her out in his dory, either fishing or exploring the coves along the shore, but the picture most vividly etched in her memory was of Captain Dad busy with his "friends."

She had been frankly curious as to why anyone as intelligent, alert, and full of humor as Captain Dad appeared to be, wanted to be a hermit. So one day she asked him, very simply, Captain Dad grunted. "Too much talkin' other places. Too many folks. Wimmin!" He spat out the last word disgustedly.

"But aren't you ever lonely?" the girl persisted. "Don't you ever want a few friends?"

"Got friends. Plenty of 'em. They wear feathers. And they ain't fickle, like the human kind of friends. No, sir! Always come when I want 'em. Just let me call, and they come."

Annie's heart raced with excitement. She sensed

that this might be something unique. She leaned forward eagerly. "I'd love to see them, Captain Dad. Won't you call them while I'm here?"

The old man shook his white head determinedly. "No. You'd frighten them. They ain't used to visitors —particularly wimmin. You'd scare 'em sick."

"How do you know?" flashed Annie, "they've never seen me."

Captain Dad puffed at his pipe and scowled at her ferociously for a long moment. Then he squinted at the sky meditatively, and chuckled. Probably he liked her spirit, and she certainly was a winsome slip of a girl sitting there on the sand, her face lit with eagerness. He knocked his pipe out on the edge of the bench and stood up.

"Set still, can ye, no matter what? Like ye do when we fish?" Annie nodded mutely, and propped her chin on her hands. The Hermit disappeared into his shack, emerging with a pail of what he explained was "candy for his friends," made of sea-moss, meal, and fish. He made what Annie described afterward as a "strange, cooing sound, amazingly loud, but not harsh." And Captain Dad had no reason to fear that she would move, for at the first sound myriads of gulls began to appear from all directions and Annie was held spellbound as they swooped and wheeled and circled, closing around Captain Dad, answering him with high, harsh cries, more and more of them, lighting on his head, his hands, his shoulders, fighting each other for his attention.

"How many can there be?" Annie whispered to herself. It seemed as though there must be thousands. The beach was dark with them. Captain Dad talked to them, rebuking them for being greedy, encouraging the smaller, weaker gulls until all the scattered food was gone and the last gull had risen on reluctant wings to swing out over the ocean.

Annie saw the sight several times afterward, but always the beauty and awe of it made her quiver.

The afternoons she had spent with Captain Dad stood out as high spots of Annie's vacations, although everything about Brewster had combined to fix it firmly in her heart.

And now it was her third (perhaps her last!) summer on the Cape. Walking swiftly along the water's edge after her solitary swim one late August afternoon, Annie knew it had been especially good for her to come here this year. Brewster was a very good place to be when one's mind had become a knotted skein of questions, doubts, fears, and ambitions. Not that she had found the answer as to what she was going to do to earn her living, but her thoughts had stopped whirling around like a kaleidoscope, and it was easier to marshal her courage and ideas here, especially here beside the sea.

The sea—here was a force she felt kinship with, always active, restless, creating new beauty. She looked at the curling breakers, tossing up lacy white fingers of spray and out over the limitless blue sweep. Its moods were very like her own, sometimes merry, sometimes almost gentle, and then gray—ruthlessly angry. And she loved the surge of the waves against her body. Somehow it gave her a feeling of strength and confidence nothing else did.

And she needed strength and courage just now. She was remembering that the end of August was in sight, and the solution of Annie Sullivan's future was not.

Oh, she had had what Captain Dad would have called several "nibbles": One of the men teachers at Perkins had written that he thought he knew of someone who might want a nursemaid for her two children, but it was nothing positive. Someone else knew of a Boston hotel where a dishwasher was wanted—Annie grimaced over that one. Miss Mary Moore wrote that she hoped Annie would decide to go to normal school and become a teacher; and Mr. Anagnos added that he would try to borrow funds for that. Annie thought that she would detest teaching ABC's all her life, and she hated the thought of borrowing. She herself had thought of selling books from door to door, but one of the girls from Perkins who had tried it had convinced her it was the world's worst job.

It was a sober girl who turned up the walk of Aunt Crocker's home. Mrs. Hopkins called to her from the kitchen.

"There's a letter waiting for you, Annie. I put it on your bureau. It's from Mr. Anagnos."

A letter—from Mr. Anagnos? For some reason Annie's hands shook as she picked up the unusually thick envelope. Her fingers made awkward work of opening the letter. Two other envelopes dropped out. They were, she saw, addressed to Mr. Anagnos. She managed to unfold the single sheet of paper, but her eyes had so blurred with excitement that she had to wait a minute or two before she could read it. Then her breath began to come hurriedly.

August 26, 1886

My dear Annie:

Please read the enclosed letters carefully, and let me know at your earliest convenience whether you would be disposed to consider favorably an offer of a position in the family of Mr. Keller as governess to his little deaf-mute and blind daughter.

I have no other information concerning the standing and responsibility of the man, save that contained in his own letters: But if you decide to be a candidate for the position, it is an easy matter to write and ask for further particulars.

I remain, dear Annie, with kind remembrances to Mrs. Hopkins,

Sincerely your friend,
M. Anagnos

Annie's heart was hammering now. Her fingers were numb as she opened the two letters signed,

23

"Arthur Keller, Tuscumbia, Alabama." She read them twice. And when she slipped them back into their envelopes the weight on her heart and the fears that had been nagging her since June were gone. Annie had found her job. Here was something new, something different, and challenging!

An excited girl whirled through the house, into the kitchen and so into Mrs. Hopkins' arms. She couldn't speak. She could only hold Mr. Anagnos' letter before Mrs. Hopkins' astonished eyes. And then suddenly they were crying and laughing together, and Annie was repeating "This is something I can do! I know I can! I know it!"

CHAPTER · 3

Journey
To
Tuscumbia

Peer as she would, Annie's near-sighted eyes could not identify Mr. Anagnos' kindly bearded face or Mrs. Hopkins' waving handkerchief among the human blobs on the snowy Boston platform, but she knew they were still there, waiting until the train pulled out, and she gripped the arm of the red plush seat hard to conquer her almost irresistible impulse to leap up and dart down the aisle and the train steps crying, "Wait! Wait! I don't want to go to Alabama. Please find me something here—in Boston."

And then the train started with a series of jerks, and Annie had begun the first lap of the journey

that would carry her to her destiny. Suddenly she
was shivering, despite her heavy gray woolen outfit.

All the girls in the cottage, as well as the faculty
of Perkins, had clustered about her this morning,
marveling at her courage and excited by the adventure that lay before her, as well as by what Mr.
Anagnos described as "the liberal salary" she would
receive—the whole of twenty-five dollars a month.
And Annie had stood in the midst of them, resplendent in her new gray outfit crowned with a
gray bonnet with bright red ribbons, and laughed
excitedly. The picture of herself as a brave young
crusader faring forth to rescue a shy, frightened
little girl from the dungeon of deaf-mute-blindness
and ignorance was very dazzling. The vision had remained while Mrs. Hopkins went with her to the
ticket agent and helped her buy the bewildering
and complicated series of tickets to Tuscumbia, Alabama, while Mr. Anagnos attended to the mysteries
of her luggage.

It lasted until she was settled in her seat and the
moment came for Annie to part from the two people
who had shown her the first kindness she had ever
discovered in the world. Then Mrs. Hopkins began
to cry as she held the girl close, and suddenly Mr.
Anagnos' voice was suspiciously husky.

And then realization shook Annie. She was going
away—over a thousand miles away from everything
and everybody she had ever known, and she had

brashly promised to undertake what had been accomplished only once or twice before: to reach and teach a child who couldn't be reached by sight or sound. If she could have found her voice at that last minute she would have begged "Let me go back," but no words came. And Mrs. Hopkins and the director were gone even as she blinked her own tears. Now she could only grip at the stiff plush and watch the city of Boston retreat past the car windows.

Gone was all the glow and sense of adventure. Gone also was the soaring sense of conviction that this was the right job for her. And that conviction had held her ever since she read Mr. Anagnos' letter that August afternoon last summer. The exaltation which had made her cry "I know I can do it!" had passed as swiftly as it came, and when it passed Annie's naturally acute mind told her that, although her acquaintance and companionship with Laura Bridgman might qualify her for the Keller position in many ways, she wasn't in the least equipped to teach a child like little Helen Keller. It was one thing to spell to Laura Bridgman and understand her finger-talk, but how did one go about reaching a child locked in a dark, silent world, in the first place? Yet she hadn't dared let this opportunity slip away. Annie remembered how she had lain awake that balmy night last August and frantically searched her mind for some inkling as to which way to look for help. And then suddenly she had recalled hearing the various teachers speak and marvel at the wonderful exactness of the reports and notes Dr. Samuel Howe and his assistants had kept on the teaching of Perkins pupils, and especially on Laura Bridgman's education. . . . The reports. That was it. They would tell her what she needed to know, wouldn't they?

Annie's letter to Mr. Anagnos had been eager. Yes, she certainly would consider the Keller position favorably. But she felt she wasn't qualified at present. Would the Perkins officials let her come back and prepare herself by studying the reports on Laura Bridgman's education?

The Perkins officials would and did. So in September Annie had returned once more to Mrs. Hopkins' friendly cottage. Everyone had been thrilled by the news. The teachers were pleased and very kind. Laura Bridgman was aquiver with joy so poignant it was almost painful. She hugged and kissed Annie again and again.

"You must teach the dear little girl many things," she spelled eagerly, "and most of all to be good and obedient!"

The girls in the cottage were delighted. Here was adventure, and their Annie was the heroine, going so far away—Alabama, and such a wonderful position.

Annie herself had pored over Dr. Howe's reports

and the notes made by Laura's other teachers. She had tried to see the Laura Bridgman who had been brought to Perkins in 1837, "a slender, delicate, agile child," bewildered by the swift change from her comfortably small New Hampshire farmhouse to the mansion that had been Perkins' first home. She had tried to picture the slight, intent young Dr. Samuel Gridley Howe, Perkins' first director, and how he had patiently worked with the child, teaching her by first pasting labels with raised letters (Laura never was taught Braille) on articles such as a key, a spoon, a book. Then the separate labels were placed in a box, and a plain key, book and spoon were given to her. She was made to feel each object and each label. It took weeks, but finally the idea flashed upon her that the letters "k-e-y" meant "key" and "b-o-o-k" meant "book," and the same thing was true of everything else. Everything had its own name. Finally Dr. Howe sent one of his teachers to learn the alphabet used by deaf mutes. She taught it to Laura by spelling the letters into the child's hand.

It wasn't easy—none of it was easy or simple—but it could be done. It sounded like bitterly hard work, but Annie Sullivan wasn't afraid of hard work.

Reading the reports had been hard work for Annie. Another person probably could have accomplished it in a third of the time, but Annie's eyes took their revenge if she read at anything approaching a normal rate. After a day of concentrated reading she would pay a toll of pain, headache, and prostration. It took her six months to absorb what she thought she needed from the reports. But during the periods when she was forced to rest her eyes she had tried to map out tentative plans for teaching little Helen, and she had assembled three embossed readers, a Braille slate, a few sewing cards and boxes of glass and wood beads.

Even the children in the cottage had wanted to have a hand in her venture. "Let's buy a doll for Miss Annie to take to Helen," one of them had proposed.

"And we'll ask Miss Laura to dress it," Lydia was inspired to add. Annie had almost been betrayed to tears when the little girls—and Laura—had crowded about her and eagerly presented their offering. It was really a beautiful doll, bought with many pennies from little banks, and few dolls could have possessed a more gorgeous wardrobe, for Laura Bridgman's needlework was a thing of art and she had taken especially loving pains with this.

" 'Doll' will be the very first word I spell to Helen," she had promised them.

Everyone had been good to her. Mr. Anagnos had loaned her money for her train fare, and given her a garnet ring, and dear Mrs. Hopkins had volunteered to get her clothes in order and pack them.

"You needn't worry your head about your clothes,

dearie," she had assured the girl. "I've made over a lavender dress I had myself when I was your age, and you've got your graduation dress—they'll do for Sunday best in the summer—and I've seen to it that the rest are good warm, substantial woolens."

What a wardrobe for a girl setting out for the balmy South in the springtime.

So, after much last-minute scurrying, the Kellers had been notified to expect her, and now a panic-shaken Annie Sullivan was aboard the train which was inexorably bearing her away from Boston this Monday morning of March 1, 1887.

The combination of the brilliant sunlight on the dazzling snow and the moving scenery brought on a stinging pain in her eyes, and Annie closed them against it, leaning her chin in her hand, ostensibly looking out of the window. It would not be the thing for a lady to appear to be sleeping in the morning. The pain probably was due to the un-healed condition of her eyes—there had been an-other operation. Her eyes had been so troublesome lately that Mr. Anagnos had insisted she see Dr. Bradford before she left for the South, and he had performed the operation only a few days ago. Per-haps she should have postponed starting, but the operation had been slight, the Kellers were expect-ing her and they had been so good about waiting.

Everyone had been good to her—the teachers, Mr. Anagnos, dear Mrs. Hopkins, Dr. Bradford, the Kellers. So why, when she was really safely on her way to what promised to be a secure position, was she so acutely conscious that she had less confidence, courage, ambition, with every turn of the wheels?

Monday was an absolutely miserable day, and snow fell so heavily Monday night that the train was two hours late in reaching Philadelphia the next morning. The cramped, weary girl wasn't in a mood to be favorably impressed by anything. "Philadelphia looks like an immense cemetery," she told Mrs. Hopkins in a note. She had to change trains there, and by the time she reached Baltimore the sun was shining and the weather so balmy her Boston clothing was torture.

Both Tuesday and Wednesday were days of misery.

"The man who sold us that ticket ought to be hanged," Annie's note cried out to Mrs. Hopkins, "and I'd be willing to act as hangman. I was obliged to change at Lynchburg, Roanoke, Chattanooga, and Knoxville. Our first stop was at Lynchburg, a dingy, dirty, rummy place."

And what would she find when she did reach Tuscumbia? Would Helen Keller be an ugly child? Annie hated ugliness. Would the illness which had taken her sight and hearing have also damaged her mind? How long would it be before the child responded at all? How much could she be taught? The thoughts that kept Annie Sullivan company on her journey were not happy ones. Finally her courage broke and she cried so desperately that one kindly conductor inquired anxiously if her folks "was dead," and tried to comfort her with sandwiches and peppermints.

It was six thirty on Wednesday afternoon before the dismal journey ended and, stiff and trembling with weariness, Annie descended to the little country platform. This was Tuscumbia, Alabama. Even before she had time to force her tired eyes to focus properly, a young man had lifted his hat courteously.

"Miss Sullivan?" the Southern drawl sounded almost foreign to her New England ears, "I am James Keller. Give me your bags. My stepmother is waiting in the carriage. If you all will kindly step over here . . ."

Suddenly Annie seemed to be gasping for breath, but she managed to move automatically beside him, and at the sight of the surprisingly young woman who was leaning forward so eagerly, "a great weight rolled off my heart," Annie confessed later, "there was so much sweetness and refinement in her."

If Kate Keller was surprised or dismayed at the appearance of the forlorn-looking, hot, and swollen-eyed young girl before her, she gave no sign, nor did she ever record it. She gave her a heart-winning smile and there was genuine welcome in her voice.

"Miss Sullivan, we are so glad to have you here at last. Someone has been meeting every train for two days."

Settled against the comfortable cushions, Annie began to relax. As they jogged along the country road lined with blossoming fruit trees, and beside fields that were fragrant with the rich smell of freshly ploughed earth, Tuscumbia seemed like Heaven itself after the dingy, stuffy trains, a good and a pleasant place to begin her life work. The ride through the spring dusk was soothing, but when Mrs. Keller pointed to a house dimly seen at the end of a long, narrow lane, and said, "Miss Sullivan, that is our home," Annie went taut with excitement. She wanted to jump out and push the ambling horse along faster. How could Mrs. Keller endure such a slow beast?

Captain Arthur Keller stood waiting in the yard to help her out of the carriage and give her a hearty handshake. "Welcome—welcome!"

Perhaps it was rude, but Annie's thoughts were focused only on one person. "Where is Helen?" she questioned breathlessly.

Captain Keller motioned toward the dusky porch. "There she is. She has known all day we were expecting someone."

Annie moved up the path, trembling now so that she could hardly control herself. Her breath came short. At the foot of the steps she stopped, afraid to look up. "Don't let her be ugly," she was praying passionately. "Oh, please, don't let her be ugly or simple-minded." And then she glanced up.

The child standing against the lighted doorway had a soiled pinafore and tumbled brown hair. You saw at a glance that she was blind, but she was far from being ugly, and although her face lacked something—mobility, perhaps soul—there was something in it that told Annie she was intelligent. Annie let go the breath she had been holding and put her foot on the bottom step. Feeling the vibration the child instantly rushed forward with such force that Annie would have been knocked backward if Captain Keller hadn't caught her. Her eager, exploring hands felt Annie's face and dress, and then found her purse. Annie let her have it, curious to see if she understood what it was. It was evident that she did, for she tried to open it. Finding it was locked, she investigated the bag carefully to see if there was a keyhole, and discovering it, she tugged at Annie's sleeve, making the motion of turning a key. Annie laughed out in joyous relief. No, Helen Keller certainly wasn't simple-minded.

"She must be very intelligent. That was very clever of her."

"Do you really think so?" Mrs. Keller's voice was wistful. She reached out and tried to rescue the bag from the little hands. Instantly the child flushed, stamped her foot, and twisted away in a temper.

35

Annie intervened, attracted Helen's attention by handing her her watch, and the storm passed. Annie had made her first conquest. Together they went into the house, and Mrs. Keller led the way upstairs to the room that would be Annie's. The lamps had been lit and to the tired girl it seemed like a very snug haven. At the window Kate Keller paused in the act of drawing the curtain, and gave Annie a poignant look.

"I hope you will be happy with us—for many years, Miss Sullivan."

Helen was tugging at her skirt, and making imperious signs to have the bag opened. Annie obeyed, letting her rummage through it. Watching her closely, she understood that the child was expecting something to eat, probably candy. Annie had noticed a trunk in the hall. She placed the child's one hand upon the trunk, the other upon her own face while she went through the motions of eating. Would the child understand?

From her delighted expression it was clear that she did. She hurried to her mother and made some rapid signs. Annie watched with mounting excitement.

"She thinks," Mrs. Keller interpreted a little apologetically, "that there is some candy for her in your trunk."

"There is, there is!" Annie cried in triumph. "That's exactly what I was trying to tell her! And she understood! She understood!"

She knew then that she had come to the right place. That she and this child would understand each other. Somehow Annie Sullivan was ready now to face the world.

CHAPTER · 4

Little Phantom

BUT SEVERAL DAYS LATER, ruefully applying a cold water compress to her bleeding mouth, Annie was beginning to think that facing the world might be an easier thing than facing one self-willed, uncontrolled little savage who flew into unpredictable rages and had just demonstrated that she was quite capable of doing real injury to anyone who opposed her. Annie had suffered the loss of two front teeth.

"She sho can be little demon when she puts her mind on it," the young Negro maid who brought the soft compresses and water, murmured with sympathy, and shook her head.

Annie sighed. She was in no mood to deny it.

The whole situation was baffling in its contradictions. She liked the Keller place. It wasn't the picturesque southern plantation with stately staircases and columns, and ballrooms she had expected; simply a plain, substantial house, but comfortable and homey, with barns and gardens, and fields to provide the family with excellent food. She liked the family. Captain Keller, a retired officer of the Confederate army, was very kind and hospitable to her. Mrs. Keller, a young woman not many years older than Annie herself, she had loved from the start with an affection which would deepen and hold for both of them all their lives. The two Keller sons by Captain Keller's first marriage, James, in his early twenties, and the teen-age Simpson, had made little impression upon her, but already she adored the rosy baby in the cradle, little Mildred. It was plain that she had come into a pleasant and refined home, and so Annie had been all the more appalled at her first breakfast with the Kellers to discover that Helen was permitted to grab at the plates as they were passed, examine them with her fingers, and pluck out the food she wanted.

Moreover, Annie learned from both Mrs. Keller and Helen's white-turbaned nurse, Viney, that more and more often force had to be used to do the simplest things, like combing the child's hair or fastening her shoes—and force brought on a rage that lasted until Helen was exhausted. It wasn't a promising outlook.

And yet, when her interest and attention could be captured she was an alert, responsive little creature. When Annie's trunk came Helen helped her unpack it, handling the articles carefully and neatly. When she discovered the doll the blind children had sent, her face broke into the first smile Annie had seen. She felt it quickly and eagerly, and hugged it close.

Remembering her promise, Annie placed one hand on the doll in the child's arm, and slowly made the letters "d-o-l-l" into her right hand. Would she catch the idea? To make sure, she used the sign she had seen Helen herself use when she wanted to claim an object. She indicated the doll, and nodded her head.

Helen looked puzzled. She felt Annie's lithe fingers, and moved them gently. Was she trying to ask for more? Annie repeated the letters. Was it possible that some dim comprehension touched the dark little mind? For as Annie held her breath the little fingers wavered through the motions of "d-o-l-l"! Helen Keller had spelled her first word! Forgotten was the half unpacked trunk. Annie stood tense with joy. And then in her excitement she made a mistake. She took back the doll. Instantly Helen's face flushed at the loss of her new treasure and she went into a temper. Annie struggled with her until she was exhausted, and then suddenly she was ashamed of her shortsightedness in bringing the tussle on herself. She sought desperately for a way to redeem herself.

Leaving the angry child, she hurried downstairs

and asked Viney for a small cake. Back in her room she caught Helen's attention, showed her the cake in one hand while she spelled "c-a-k-e" with the other. Helen snatched at the cake, but Annie held it firmly while she patted her hand encouragingly. And once again something penetrated the child's consciousness, for she made the letters swiftly and ate the cake in a hurry. Then Annie offered her the doll again, and touched her fingers. What would happen now? What happened was like a miracle. Helen frowned, but slowly her fingers moved to spell "d-o-l." Annie made the second "l" for her, and placed the doll in her arms. Helen turned and groped her way from the room. She would have nothing to do with Annie the rest of the day.

But Annie, going about the remainder of her unpacking, and settling herself in the first room she could call her own, was in a state of exultation. She had broken through the barrier to the child's consciousness. She knew now that Helen Keller was an eager, intelligent human being and not a groping defective.

The next day she brought out her kindergarten materials, and showed Helen how to do one of the little sewing cards. Helen was pleased when she felt the little holes, and screamed with delight when she discovered she had achieved something she could feel. She did the card surprisingly well, and Annie praised her by patting her head, and then decided to try another word. She tapped the card, and then spelled the word into Helen's hand, as she had "doll" and "cake" the day before.

Helen imitated the "c-a—" and paused, cocking her head. Then she made her sign for eating, and pointed downward, and pushed Annie toward the door. Annie supplied the other two letters, "k-e," and laughing, went in search of another cake. How bright the little thing was. By Dr. Howe's report it had taken weeks before he was sure Laura Bridgman sensed connections between words.

Even with her ingenious sign language Helen showed that she was exceptional. Only that morning Annie had seen her tugging at her mother's skirts as Mrs. Keller went about her work, and then when she knew she had her mother's attention, go through the motions of turning a handle and shivering. Her motions were so expressive Annie hadn't needed Mrs. Keller's laughing explanation, "She wants ice cream for dinner."

And at dinner she had asked for bread and butter by going through the perfectly understandable motions of slicing bread and buttering it.

But perhaps one had to see her out-of-doors, feeling her way slowly but fearlessly around the sheds and stables, the garden and the farm to see to what an astonishing degree this silent, sightless child had established communion with things about her. Eager to learn her haunts and habits, Annie had followed her out into the balmy spring morning the day after Annie's arrival. (Was it possible that only four days before she had been almost snow-bound on the train to Philadelphia?) And as she watched the little figure making its way by means of hedges, bushes, and trees, she grew more and more astounded. Helen would stop, sniff the air, and then nod in apparent satisfaction, and proceed.

With Annie at her heels she groped her way to where the cows were being milked. Evidently she was no stranger to the place, for the milkers showed no surprise, even when Helen ran her hands over the nearest cow. The animal gave her an indignant swish of its tail, but Helen stood her ground, and Annie marveled. One of the farm hands took her hand and led her to the horses' stable. He lifted her and she petted one of the horses with evident delight.

Outside once more, Helen felt her way along the boxwood hedge until she came to the kitchen garden. And here, by some means known only to herself, she discovered another person, a grinning, be-ribboned little Negro girl a year or two older than she was. Mrs. Keller had pointed the child out to Annie as Martha Washington, the daughter of the cook, one of the few children not afraid of Helen, and her constant companion.

Helen had thrown her arms around the little girl, and then had begun tugging at her sleeve and squat-

ting on the ground to make curious gestures with
both hands. Martha Washington nodded vigorously
and grinned wider.

"What is she saying?" Annie had been trying to
follow the gestures, but she was completely baffled.

"She's saying she wants to go huntin' for guinea-
hen eggs," Martha explained with a little bob. "See?
Like this—" she doubled her little brown hands into
fists and put them on the ground. "Guinea-bird, she
like to lay eggs in high grass, and Helen, she sho
love to hunt for them. Yes, honey we go." Instinctively she addressed Helen aloud in answer to a
more insistent tug at her arm.

"Her fists make the eggs in the grass," Annie said
to herself. "That really is clever."

"Oh, yes, ma'am." Martha agreed. "Helen sho is
smart."

She was more than that, Annie thought as she
followed the two little girls through the high grass.
She had a gift most blind children lack—an undaunted, fearless spirit, and an unquenched love of
activity. Many blind children, the smaller ones especially, are uncertain, fearful, willing to stay in
one place. Some blind babies have difficulty in
learning to walk. Annie had seen blind children at
Perkins who had to be taught how to play. Yet
here was a sturdy little soul who had grown up
from a silent babyhood as well as a dark one, and
was as active, tireless, and mischievous as any normal six-and-a-half child would be.

Annie smiled to herself at the memory of her expectation of a "pale, delicate, timid child." As she had told Mrs. Hopkins in the letter she was writing, "there is nothing delicate about Helen! She is large, strong, and ruddy, and as unrestrained in her movements as a young colt."

And then she suddenly saw something that made her laugh outright. The little girls evidently had come upon a nest of eggs. They were screaming with delight, and Annie didn't need Martha's interpretation of Helen's expressive gestures. Helen was informing Martha that she, Helen, would carry the eggs home in her pinafore. Martha might stumble and break them.

Back at the house, with the eggs disposed of safely, the little girls sat on the kitchen steps and fed the turkeys gobbling around them. Annie noticed they pecked the grain directly from Helen's hand, and marveled once again. The sight was so incredible for anyone who had known blind children—and been one herself. Intelligent and fearless as Helen certainly was, there was something more. In back of Helen there was a wonderful family— especially a mother wise and patient and strong enough to let her baby go exploring and learn by experience just as other babies did, rather than hold her back for fear she would be hurt.

She told Mrs. Keller so as they sat together after Helen's bedtime. Mrs. Keller shook her head, with the tears filling her eyes. Until Annie came she had never dared confess to anyone how bitter the years of Helen's babyhood had been.

"She was such a beautiful baby, Miss Annie, and with such sharp eyes. She could see a needle where no one else could. And the day she was a year old she slipped off my lap and fairly ran toward a sunbeam. She was beginning to talk, too. And then when she was nineteen months old she was ill. We still don't know what it was. The doctors called it 'acute congestion of stomach and brain.' I discovered when I was bathing her that she was blind, and later—she didn't turn her head—even when we screamed. But I never believed her brain was damaged—do you?"

Annie's head moved quickly and emphatically. "No, Mrs. Keller! It certainly isn't. I've seen feebleminded persons. I know."

"Some of our relatives told us she was defective, that we should put her away. But a cousin of the Captain's has always claimed she had more sense than any of the other Kellers if there only is a way to get at her mind."

Annie swallowed hard. "There is, dear Mrs. Keller; it's been done before. I lived with Laura Bridgman, and she has studied a good many things; even geometry and science. She's quite a wonderful person."

"It was reading about her in Dickens' *American Notes* that gave me my first hope. And then I remembered that Dr. Howe was dead, and perhaps his methods had died with him. And then President Cleveland made my husband a marshall of Alabama, and he used his first salary to take Helen to an oculist we'd heard of in Baltimore." She bit her lip. "It was hopeless, but he said he was sure she could be educated, and he advised us to see Dr. Alexander Graham Bell in Washington."

"Dr. Alexander Graham Bell?" Annie interrupted, "I thought—the telephone—I thought he was an inventor."

Mrs. Keller nodded. "That's right, but before that he taught the deaf. His own wife is deaf. Well, we went to Washington, and Dr. Bell—he is the greatest and the kindest man I've met." Her voice failed her on the last words, and she looked away for a second. "He held Helen on his knee, and they understood each other at once. He said she was a very bright child, and of course she could be educated, and advised my husband to write to the Perkins Institution. And oh, Miss Annie, it was the gladdest day of our lives when Mr. Anagnos wrote that you would come to us."

Annie's throat tightened. All the despair of the months and years of helpless waiting and hoping were in Kate Keller's eyes.

"I'll do my best for you and Helen," she promised soberly. "I love her already. And she's very quick at learning anything new." She laughed a little. "Remember the 'cake'—'card' incident, and how well she did the sewing-cards and the beads?"

Helen's mother asked how Annie was going to go about teaching her. Which was a very good question, for Annie had very hazy and short-range plans, at present. She explained that the important thing would be to make Helen understand that everything in the world had a name. She planned to give her objects like the cake: card, doll, cup, spoon— familiar things—and spell the words to her until Helen linked the word with the object and used it herself without mistake. She explained that each letter of the alphabet could be made by a motion of the fingers in the alphabet used by the deaf, and demonstrated by spelling the name Helen Keller.

This alphabet was easily learned by anyone, Annie explained. Later Helen would learn to read and write Braille, and also to write by pencil. She could be taught arithmetic and practically anything else by Braille.

The dainty jacket for baby Mildred dropped into Kate Keller's lap. Hope she hadn't known for five years gleamed in her face.

"You can really do all that, Miss Annie? I really will talk to my little girl and know what she thinks? What does she think?"

What, indeed, were little Helen Keller's thoughts at this period? She herself cannot say. It is very hard to imagine thoughts without words. And Helen

Keller had no words. She remembers experiences. She remembers wading through a mass of papers to find her father (he was a newspaper editor) holding something before his face that puzzled her very much. She tried holding the thing before her own face, and even put on his spectacles, but it didn't solve the mystery. She remembers that she and Martha Washington stole a freshly-iced cake and took it to the woodpile to eat. She remembers being angry at finding her baby sister asleep in the cradle she used for her doll, and trying to upset the cradle. She remembers having locked her mother in a pantry, and setting her apron on fire by holding it over an open fire. And she remembers the journey to Baltimore to the oculist and then on to Washington very vividly.

Everyone on the trains was very good to her. One passenger gave her a box of shells to play with; her father punched holes in them and she strung them as a necklace. The conductor let her hold fast to his coattail as he went through the car taking tickets, and afterward he gave her his punch to play with. Perhaps the most amazing incident of the trip came when an aunt made her a rag doll out of towels, a funny, floppy, formless thing. Oddly, it was the lack of eyes which attracted little Helen's attention. She kept pointing to the doll's face and then to her own eyes, but no one could suggest a way to supply the doll with eyes. Finally Helen's

own face lighted, and she scrambled from her seat
and felt her way to where an aunt was seated. She
felt under the seat till she found the cloak her aunt
had been wearing during the journey. The cloak
was trimmed with large beads. Helen's strong little
fingers pulled off two beads and indicated the doll's
face. When they were sewn in place she hopped up
and down in joy.

She could not know Dr. Chisholm's verdict, or the
heavy hearts with which her parents took her to
Washington. But somehow as she sat on Dr. Bell's
knee, she did know that here was someone who
understood her, and he was the first person outside
her family with whom she felt an instinctive communication. Later she was to call him "my oldest
friend."

What thoughts did she have in the five years she
wandered in complete isolation? She said years later
that she "was like a ship in a dense fog, groping its
way without compass or sounding-line." And that
she lived in "a conscious time of nothingness. I did
not know that I knew aught or that I lived or acted.
I had neither will nor intellect. . . . I had no power
of thought." She also called herself a "Phantom in
a No-World."

What thoughts she had must have been formless
and shadowy, but she was certainly aware of many
things, and she was perfectly aware that she was
different from other people. She realized that they

did not use signs and gestures as she did. She would stand between two people, with her fingers on their moving lips, and then move her own in a futile attempt to be like them.

It must have been this urgent need for understanding others and communicating with them that brought on the storms that had become so frequent by the time Annie Sullivan reached Tuscumbia. Probably they were not temper-tantrums, but paroxysms of grief and despair at the unyielding barriers that were keeping her growing mind imprisoned. After she was exhausted she would feel her way along the boxwood hedge to the garden, and then fling her storm-shaken little body down among the flowers to be soothed by their coolness and sweetness.

It was in one of these paroxysms that her fists flew so violently that Annie lost her two front teeth. Annie was at low ebb herself that day. Her eyes were painful and inflamed. She did not know how to cope with a headstrong little savage who had never been disciplined, and whose family refused to have her curbed in any way. She had thought to reach the child by love, but Helen was too wild and uncontrolled and unreachable to recognize or understand love. Annie must do something else, and do it soon.

Perhaps she thought of another blind, unmanageable, untaught child, and the time and patience it had taken to gentle her. At any rate she lifted her head and tried to forget her ruined mouth.

I must get the child away from her family, she thought. That's the first thing. I'll have a good, frank talk with Mrs. Keller.

CHAPTER · 5

First Rung

AND THEN MATTERS CAME to a sudden and violent climax the next morning. Perhaps it was because she was discouraged, disappointed, and tense at the prospect of proposing to Mrs. Keller that Helen should be separated from her family temporarily, but Annie watched with increasing distaste as Helen investigated the plates as they were passed. As her own plate was passed to her, she warded off the invading little hands. Instantly the child's face darkened. She pinched Annie. Annie slapped her hand. That was enough to set off Helen's temper explosion. She screamed and then made another lunge at Annie's plate. Only too conscious of the family's shocked and disapproving expressions, Annie slapped the prowling hand again. Mrs. Keller opened her lips, and then shook her head. The

tears rolled down her cheeks. She stood up, and
one after another the family followed her example
and left the room.

Annie rose too, but she only went far enough to
close and lock the door. Her own tears came, but
forlorn and empty as she felt, she forced herself to
sit down and resume her breakfast, although the
food choked her. What was to be the outcome? She
had never meant it to be like this. She had meant
to win Helen by love and gentleness, but that hadn't
worked. Helen accepted everything as a matter of
course. She actually refused to be loved. Everyone
in the family, especially her father, hated to see her
cry; therefore she had never been disciplined or con-
trolled, and if she ever failed to get anything she
wanted it was only because she couldn't make herself understood. The only thing she could understand and respect was something stronger than herself. Annie hoped she was the stronger. And once
it was begun, she would finish this battle.

And it was a battle. Helen was lying on the floor,
screaming her unearthly screams, kicking and trying
to get Annie's chair from under her. Annie held fast.
Finally the child scrambled to her feet to see what
Annie was doing. When she saw she was trying to
eat, she once again tried to snatch the food. Annie
slapped her again. The child felt her way around
the table. She seemed bewildered at the empty
chairs, but she came back to her own chair and

began eating her own breakfast—with her fingers. Annie gave her a spoon, which Helen threw on the floor. Annie made her pick it up, held the spoon firmly in the child's hand and compelled her to eat with it. A surprised expression crossed Helen's face, but she caught the idea and finished her breakfast quietly. Then they had another tussle over folding her napkin. When it was folded, Helen tossed it on the floor. Annie set her teeth and despite the renewed kicking and screaming, made her pick it up and fold it all over again. Finally she let the child out into the warm sunshine and then, trembling and half sick, she managed to get to her own room, where she threw herself in a tumbled heap on her bed to cry until very exhaustion made her cease.

Oh, it was no use. She had failed. Captain Keller would certainly ask her to pack. And if he didn't, how could she—how could anyone—*reach* such a child?

Perhaps she fell into a sleep that verged on stupor. And then a gentle voice was saying, "Miss Annie? May I come in?"

Annie struggled to sit up and with a voice still thick with tears croaked "Y-yes, c-come in." It was Mrs. Keller, and she was probably bringing the family's decision for her return to Boston.

Kate Keller came in, stood looking at the forlorn figure for a moment, then sat down on the wide bed and put her arms around Annie. "Oh, my dear Miss

Annie, I am so sorry about this morning! How can we help you? We want to do our best for our little girl, but how can we do it?"

Annie swallowed, reached for her sodden handkerchief, and gratefully accepted the fresh one Mrs. Keller was offering. She looked into the anxious face and then began speaking, slowly, groping for the right words.

"I think she must be sent away from the family, for a while——"

"Sent away!" Helen's mother drew back.

Annie nodded. "Yes. For a few weeks at least. Oh, don't you see, Mrs. Keller? You—all her family have always allowed her to do exactly as she pleased. She has tyrannized over all of you, even the servants. She has these rages over everything now, and you give in for the sake of peace. I can't teach her language or anything else until she learns to obey me. She must learn to depend upon me, and to obey me and love me, before I can make any headway. As long as she thinks her family are with her, it's no use. Will you let me take her away for just a little while?"

Mrs. Keller hesitated a long time. Annie could tell from her expression that a struggle was tearing her two ways. Then she looked up, and her smile was wistful. "I will certainly think about it and see what Captain Keller says, Miss Annie."

Annie was dubious about Captain Keller's reaction, but when he asked her to come into his den with Mrs. Keller that evening, his first words left her limp with surprised delight.

"I think you may have an excellent plan, Miss Annie," he said cordially. "Now it happens that there is a little garden house of ours, about a quarter of a mile from here, near Ivy Green, our family plantation. We can get that ready for you. Helen has been there often, but of course you would be alone with her. Would you have objections to our looking in at the windows each day to see how you are getting on? Helen need know nothing of our visits."

"Oh, no, sir!" Annie said fervently. "May we go soon?"

"Good. Why, yes, I think it can be arranged quickly enough." He patted her hand. "My dear young woman, we know you are trying to help us."

The little house to which they were taken seemed to Annie like a genuine bit of Paradise. There was one large square room with a great fireplace and a wonderful bay window, and a smaller room where the little Negro boy, Percy, who was to do their chores, would sleep. There was a large porch, covered with vines so thick that they had to be parted to see the garden beyond. Their meals would be brought from the "big house," Ivy Green, where Captain Keller's relatives lived, so Annie would be completely free to devote all her attention to Helen.

The little house might be a small paradise, but its two occupants were in no heavenly state of mind, not for the first couple of days at least. Separated from her family and familiar surroundings, Helen fell into a paroxysm of combined terror and anger and expressed it in the only way she knew, by kicking and screaming. Annie stood by helpless and leadenhearted. When supper was brought, Helen grew calmer and brighter and ate heartily, and then played with her dolls; when Annie indicated it was bedtime, she allowed herself to be undressed and tucked in readily enough. But when she felt Annie get in beside her, it was another matter. Helen jumped out the other side. Annie picked her up and put her back. Helen rolled out again. The ordeal lasted for two hours.

"I've never seen such strength and endurance in a child," Annie wrote to Mrs. Hopkins, "but fortunately for us both, I am a little stronger."

Eventually Helen surrendered and lay on the edge of the bed, a sobbing curled-up little girl, and Annie lay on her side of the bed, weary in both mind and body, and filled with tormenting doubts.

Poor little girl, it wasn't her fault she was so locked from all human communication and understanding. Annie suddenly remembered what Dr. Howe had said about Laura Bridgman: ". . . She was like a person alone and helpless in a deep, dark, still pit, and I was letting down a cord and dangling it about in hopes that she might find it, and seize it by chance, and be drawn up into the light of day and human society."

How soon would Helen find the cord that Annie was trying to let down to her?

In the morning Captain Keller looked through the window on his way to his newspaper office, and Annie realized all too well that no father could consider what he saw encouraging. It was mid-morning, and Helen was sitting in the middle of the floor, a bundle of misery, with her clothes scattered about her, having fought off all Annie's attempts to dress her. Whatever he was thinking, the father concealed it from Annie, and only greeted her with Southern courtesy, but her heart sank as she saw the haggard look on his face as he turned away.

And indeed Annie was perilously close to being sent back to Perkins in defeat, for Captain Keller stopped at Ivy Green and announced to his cousin, "Leila, I've a good mind to send that Yankee girl straight back to Boston."

But Leila Lassiter had made a clearer appraisal of the situation. "Give her a real chance to prove what she's doing, Arthur," she urged. "I think she's Helen's only hope."

Helen was subdued and baffled that day. She played with her dolls, went often to the door as though she was expecting someone, touched her cheek, which was her sign for her mother, and then shook her head sadly. She had as little as possible to do with Annie.

How utterly baffled and abandoned she must feel,

thought Annie, watching her. She couldn't be blamed if her family's indulgence and lack of discipline had made this separation imperative—and possibly the Kellers couldn't be blamed, either. It is difficult to devise punishments for a child with whom you can't communicate. Because of the absolute freedom she was accustomed to, Helen had, as Annie had written to Mrs. Hopkins, none of the nervous habits that were so distressing in blind children. Her freedom and her fearlessness would be very valuable to her when she could really knowingly take part in the world about her. But how am I going to teach her obedience and self control without breaking her wonderful spirit, thought Annie.

How indeed? Here was a problem that would have baffled and dismayed an older and much more experienced teacher than Annie, and Annie faced it with youth and inexperience. She was still a month short of being twenty-one.

How and when the thing happened no one concerned ever knew, but suddenly it dawned upon Helen's dark little mind that this person with her was no ogre who had snatched her away from her family for some cruel purpose, but someone whose touch was gentle and friendly, who knew more things even than her mother, and who wanted to show her how to do them. Here was someone to be trusted, depended upon—and more, to be obeyed.

Under Annie's guidance she made an apron for

her doll, and it was a good apron. She learned to crochet, and when she'd made a chain long enough to reach across the room she chuckled and held it lovingly against her cheek. And Annie could write excitedly to Mrs. Hopkins:

March 20, 1887

My heart is singing for joy this morning! The light of understanding has shone upon my little pupil, and behold all things are changed.

The wild little creature of two weeks ago has been transformed into a gentle child. She is sitting beside me as I write, serene and happy, crocheting a long red chain of Scotch wool. . . . She lets me kiss her now, and when she is in a particularly gentle mood, she will sit in my lap. . . . The great step—the step that counts —has been taken. The little savage has learned her first lesson in obedience. Already people remark the difference in Helen. Her father looks in on us morning and evening, and sees her contentedly stringing her beads and sewing, and exclaims, "How quiet she is!" When I first came her movements were so insistent that one always felt there was something unnatural and weird about her.

Helen was learning to spell more words, too. When Annie gave her objects she had had before, she identified them quickly, but it was evident that she didn't associate words with her own desires, for when she wanted milk or cake, she used her old gestures for them, rather than spell the words themselves. But she liked the finger play, and she was growing very deft with it.

One day Captain Keller brought Belle, one of the Keller setters with him, wondering whether Helen would recognize her. The dog crouched in the corner of the room, making Annie surmise she didn't have too happy memories of her small mistress. Helen had been giving one of her dolls a bath, but suddenly she stopped, sniffed, and then dumped the doll into the washbasin and felt her way around the room. It was evident that she did recognize Belle, for she gave a little cry of joy, dropped on her knees and hugged her hard. Then she stooped and began to work one paw. Neither Captain Keller nor Annie could guess what was in her mind, until they saw the little fingers flutter in the motions that spell "d-o-l-l."

Helen was trying to teach the dog to spell.

CHAPTER · 6

W–A–T–E–R!

THEY STAYED IN THE LITTLE GARDEN HOUSE two weeks. Annie wished it might have been longer, but Captain Keller said he thought Helen was homesick. The truth probably was that her parents were homesick for Helen.

Everyone noticed and exclaimed over the improvement in the child. Her face was growing more expressive every day; the wild tantrums were vanishing; she was more affectionate; even though she hadn't quite found the use of words, it was obvious that her eager mind was at work. One day when she was playing in the garden she dug a hole, and to Annie's astonishment, buried her doll. But then by her expressive pantomime she showed Annie that she expected the doll to grow as big as Annie. "You have no idea how cunning she is," she exclaimed to Mrs. Hopkins.

Annie was more confident now that she was on

the right track. Her success in the garden house had impressed the Kellers, and they had agreed to give her a free hand in anything she wanted to do. Helen even slept with her now, because Annie wanted her to feel dependent upon her, and besides,

I find it much easier to teach her things at odd moments than at set times. . . . *I spell into her hand everything that we do all day long, even though as yet she doesn't know what the spelling means.*

And then, on a certain exquisite, fragrance-filled April morning, just a month and two days after she had arrived in Tuscumbia, April 5, 1887—neither Annie nor Helen could ever forget the day or the date—something happened that sent a wildly excited Annie flying to her room to snatch up her writing desk with fingers that trembled so that they scattered the paper and stamps in all directions. With her heart pounding in her throat she sat down to pour out her joyous tidings to Mrs. Hopkins:

I must write you a line this morning because something very important has happened. Helen has learned that *everything has a name, and that the manual alphabet is the key to everything she wants to know.*

In a previous letter I wrote you that "mug" and "milk" had given Helen more trouble than all the rest. She didn't know the word for "drink" but she went through the pantomime of drinking whenever she spelled "mug" or "milk." This morning while she was

washing she wanted to know the name for "water." . . .
I spelled it, and thought no more about it, until after
breakfast. Then it occurred to me that with the help of
this new word I might straighten out the "mug-milk"
difficulty. We went out to the pump house and I made
Helen hold her hand under the spout while I pumped.
I spelled "w-a-t-e-r" into her free hand. . . . The word
coming so close upon the sensation of cold water rushing over her hand seemed to startle her. She dropped
the mug and stood transfixed. A new light came into her
face. She spelled "water" several times. Then she
dropped to the ground and asked its name. She pointed
to the pump and the trellis, and then suddenly turning
around she asked my name. I spelled "teacher." Just
then the nurse brought Helen's baby sister into the
pump house, and Helen spelled "baby" and pointed to
the nurse.

All the way back to the house Helen was excited
and joyous. She touched every object she could
reach, and pulled at Annie's sleeve to ask its name.
Annie's fingers trembled so she could barely spell
things. She gasped out the wonderful news to Mrs.
Keller and then sped upstairs to begin her letter
to Mrs. Hopkins. Helen Keller had found the cord
that would take her out of her own "deep, dark,
still pit back into human society."

Even as she wrote, Helen was darting around the
room, her face more joyous than any face Annie had
ever seen, touching familiar objects and spelling
their newly-found names rapidly in the air—"door,"

65

"bed," "candy," and then over and over the word that was to become the loveliest word of all to her, "teacher." She came close to Annie, hovering over her, touching her hair and her cheek gently, while her fingers went through the letters "t-e-a-c-h-e-r" again and again. Annie dropped her pen and hugged the child tightly.

It was a wonderful day. Helen couldn't get enough of new words. Everywhere she went—everything she touched, there was the eager touch on Annie's hand, and when Annie had supplied the word the child's whole body seemed to quiver with happiness. There were verbs now as well as nouns —"run," "sit," "walk," and commands like "go," "come," "give." Helen was drinking up words as thirstily as she would water on a hot day.

By the time night came Annie's fingers were weary, but the weariness was actually pleasant as she saw Kate Keller's face when Helen climbed into her lap and spelled "Mother."

Indeed you could feel the joy in the very atmosphere of the Keller house. Even the servants went about grinning from ear to ear, or stood watching Helen with positive awe. As for her father, he could only follow his little daughter wherever she went, and feast his eyes upon her tiny moving fingers.

When Helen's bedtime arrived, and Annie stood up to bid the family good night, Captain Keller rose from his chair and came across the room to her. He tried to say something, but his voice did not come, and Annie choked a little herself as she answered the convulsive grip of his hand: "Thank you, sir."

Annie's cup had been full to running over that day. For once, she thought as she made her own preparations for bed, she couldn't wish for anything more!

But the next morning her letter to Mrs. Hopkins carried a postscript:

"Last night when I got in bed, Helen stole into my arms of her own accord and kissed me for the first time, and I thought my heart would burst, so full was it of joy!"

And Helen later wrote of that same night: "It would have been difficult to find a happier child than I was as I lay in my bed at the close of that eventful day and lived over the joys it had brought me, and for the first time longed for a new day to come."

CHAPTER · 7

"More Words—
Much Words!"

ANNIE WAS WAKENED the next morning by an insistent tugging at her hand. Helen was standing beside her, her clothes clutched in one hand, pulling at her bedfellow with the other until she was satisfied that Annie was awake. Then she began to use very emphatic pantomime to inform her teacher that it was high time to be up and about. Annie laughed out and impulsively swept the little figure in its voluminous nightgown into her arms for a swift hug. How good it was to have the little thing instinctively come to her. And how marvelous to see the change from a restless, excitable half-human being into this responsive child whose face was beginning to reflect thoughts and ideas.

And when Helen's arms found Annie's neck and

she kissed her in response to Teacher's greeting, Annie Sullivan's heart overflowed.

Even the business of bathing and dressing Helen was a far cry from the exhausting ordeal it had been a fortnight or so before. Annie was glad that she had told Mrs. Keller she didn't want a nurse for Helen, that she wanted the child to depend upon her for everything, for this morning Helen's flying fingers were demanding the names for every article Annie used and each piece of clothing she put on, a process which would have been definitely impeded if a nurse had been handling the child. It took a little longer, but Helen's eager face and increasing vocabulary were the things that counted. Annie stood back and surveyed her handiwork. Really, in her crisply-fresh pinafore, with her hair prettily combed, and her intelligent face becoming expressive as her ideas and thoughts struggled to be born, little Helen Keller was adorable.

Suddenly missing Annie's friendly touch, Helen frowned and put out questioning hands. Annie took one and spelled: "Go down—eat."

Helen nodded enthusiastically and made her way rapidly to the stairs. At the top step she hesitated, not, as Annie knew, from any fear, for she fearlessly ran up and down the flight all day long, but a thought seemed to have crossed her mind. There was a peculiarly sweet expression on the little face turned to Annie as the child found her teacher's hand and slipped her own into it confidingly.

And so they descended the stairs and crossed the wide hall into the dining room, and even near-sighted Annie couldn't miss the expressions of joy, amazement and sheer unbelief that crossed the faces of the various members of the Keller family as she and her charge entered the room. And she wouldn't have been human if she hadn't experienced a pleased glow. She knew everyone was really awed by the contrast between the uncontrollable small savage of less than a month ago and this radiant, human little girl. But even Annie shared their astonishment as Helen made her way around the table, touching the people present, and then spelling each name correctly. It seemed unbelievable that she not only remembered the names she had been told yesterday, but that she could and did associate them with the right persons.

"She *knows* us! She knows who we are!" choked Mrs. Keller. "Oh, Miss Annie, you can't know—there's no way for you to know—what that means! She'll be able to understand us, and be a real part of us! It's—it's"—she wiped her eyes and fought against betraying her emotions—"it's the most marvelous thing I could ever have prayed to happen!"

And from his end of the table Captain Keller was saying heartily, "It's an actual miracle—and this is only the beginning for her! If you have done so much for Helen in just these few days, and she's learned with such astonishing rapidity, what *will* she be able to accomplish? How far will she have the capacity to go?"

It was a joyous question, and a joyful meal, probably the happiest the Kellers had known in years, although they actually ate very little food, since their fascinated attention was fixed on Helen. Even the Negro servants stood still, watching her with their eyes rolling in awe.

"I've always maintained that child has more sense than all the rest of us Kellers put together, if there was some way of getting at her brain!" declared Captain Keller's sister in a satisfied voice. "That child has a better mind than you think!"

"But it took Miss Annie to know how to reach it," Mrs. Keller reminded her.

Small wonder that the entire Keller household held its breath over the sight of this happy-faced, prettily-dressed-and-combed little Helen contentedly feeding herself with the spoon Annie had placed in her hand. Here was one victory which this Confederate family was glad to see won by a Yankee.

Annie's cheeks flushed with the quick thrill of her first triumphs and the Kellers' praise, but later, when she had taken Helen out into the sunny, old-fashioned garden for her usual morning playtime, the memory of Captain Keller's exultant question hammered at her mind with sobering force: "What will she be able to accomplish? How far will she have the capacity to go?" She thought of Laura Bridgman: Laura, who had had the advantage of being taught by Dr. Howe and the best teachers he could find for her, wiser and better trained people than Annie could ever hope to be; and yet—Annie was forced to admit the fact—Laura lived a strange, isolated life. She was happy, and she was useful with her sewing, knitting and crocheting, yes, but she had never been able to cope with the ordinary, workaday world. Past fifty now, she still lived on in the haven of the school where she had been since she was seven years old. She had tried living at home with her family after her education had been finished, but that had been a pathetic and frightening failure. Why? Was that the way it had to be in cases like Laura Bridgman and Helen Keller? Did that have to be Helen's fate: living in a secluded, protected corner—an isolated, strange person? The thought caught at Annie's heart.

Helen came and pulled at her hand and asked the name of the flower she had just plucked. Annie spelled it for her absently while her thoughts tumbled on. Words. Of course Helen could learn words. She was learning with breathtaking speed. But mere words aren't language. Could she learn the ebb and flow of ordinary conversation? Despite all her teachers Laura Bridgman never had acquired it. Examples of her talk and writing flashed across Annie's mind:

Speaking of one of the teachers she had said, "I

do not trust that she would have so perfect health and strength as myself, as it is very unnatural to her."

And speaking of a fine day, she remarked, "I enjoyed it much. It reminded me of my best Father in Heaven. He was extremely benevolent so as to dispatch the sun and such a delightful day."

Once when she was writing of a teacher who had left Perkins, she wrote to her mother:

She gave me a very beautiful and pure breastpin, just before I parted from her . . . I love her half as much as if she was my wife.

Was that the best that could be expected of Helen? Or was it the way Laura had been taught? Annie remembered the story of how Laura had once baffled everybody by asking, "Is it derivative today?" Finally it was discovered that Dr. Howe had told her "rain" was a primary word, and "rainy" a derivative word, so of course poor Laura had thought she was asking "Is it rainy?"

How did a normal child learn language anyway?

Something suddenly brushed Annie's knee gently, and she looked down into the roguish face of Helen's fifteen-month-old cousin. Annie bent and kissed her quickly. Normal babies were new and fascinating to Annie, and she found both Mildred and this mite enchanting. She was half sorry when the child's Negro nurse came hurrying up.

"Go along wif you now, Little Honey! Run along and smell de flowers, and quit bothering Miss Annie. And doan' you pester Helen none."

"She wasn't bothering me," Annie protested. She smiled again and waved as the baby scampered away, exploring the flowers as she went, but obediently avoiding the path that would have led her past the spot where Helen and Martha Washington were busily digging holes. Annie's thoughts turned back to Laura Bridgman, and then suddenly stopped. It was as though an electric signal had flashed in her brain. She stared after the baby. The child had obeyed her mammy. She had obeyed her because she understood what had been said. And Annie had seen that happen several times before. Her breath began to come a little short. She called the child's name. The baby turned her head inquiringly, and Annie held out her arms invitingly.

"Come?" she said coaxingly, "Will you come over here?"

The child knew Annie. They had become friends days before. She seemed to consider for a second, and then decided to accept the invitation. Reaching the bench where Annie sat, she favored her with an enchanting smile, and Annie hugged her. Now she began the experiment that had leapt into her mind.

"Where is baby's ear?" she asked. Instantly the child pointed to it. "Fine!" Annie agreed. "Now where's the little rogue?"

Two tiny hands went up to cover the small face, and only the twinkling blue eyes peeped out between the spread fingers. When Annie applauded and asked for a kiss, she received it. She made one final test. Picking a nearby rose, she stripped it of its thorns, and put it into the baby's hand. "Take it to Mamma," she suggested, and watched. Almost she could see the thought beginning to turn in the small mind. The baby paused, then turned and tugged at her nurse's apron, and pattered off in the direction of the house.

"She understood everything, didn't she?" Annie cried gleefully to the slower-moving nurse. The woman gave her a half-patronizing, half-scornful glance.

"Course Little Honey understan'. She sho do."

Annie watched them depart and then looked toward Helen with a rising excitement. Her experiment had worked. It was perfectly evident that long before the baby could use sentences herself she understood what they meant. That was the key: Babies weren't *taught* language. They absorbed it like little sponges because words were whirling around them all day long. Very well, words would whirl around Helen all day long too.

I will talk into her hand just as we talk into the baby's ears. Annie resolved on a sudden inspiration. I shall use complete sentences in talking to her, and encourage everybody else to do so, and by and by she'll know and use all the words herself.

Was that the explanation of Laura Bridgman's failure to acquire idiomatic English? Because her teachers had been so zealously careful to define each and every word they used to her, and spelled in brief, staccato sentences? All the reports showed that Laura had been taught by a very carefully prepared program, and Annie's own experiences with her told her she was an exceptionally intelligent woman.

Helen had left Martha, and was feeling her way to Annie by means of the boxwood hedge. She had captured a curious bug, and pulling at her teacher's sleeve, demanded its name.

Annie spelled "bug," and glanced at her watch. It was wonderful here in the garden, but it was the hour for Helen's "lesson" with new words, and after that her knitting or sewing stint. Annie sighed. She had once confessed to Mrs. Hopkins that she personally considered knitting and crocheting inventions of the devil, and she'd "rather break stones in the highway than hem a handkerchief." She rose reluctantly and started to tell Helen they were returning to the house, and then she stopped short. It was spring out here, glorious, fragrant, sunny, and a healthy, active child like Helen and the spring were made for each other. Helen was happy and contented. She was beginning to find the garden and the farm an exciting, enchanting place. Out here her curiosity made her clamor for more and more words. Wasn't it utterly absurd to drag her into the house and force her to sit in her little chair at her little table, feeling objects like a spoon or a dish in which she wasn't interested, when she was fairly quivering with excitement to learn about everything she was encountering by touch and smell in this springtime world?

Standing there in the Keller garden Annie Sullivan suddenly made the decision that saved Helen Keller from the squirrel-cage life Laura Bridgman and many another handicapped person has lived: She tossed away all her preconceived plans for formal "lessons." Hereafter there would be no set time for forcing Helen to sit at a little table learning special words or doing routine work. She would come and go and do and play without knowing she was doing something important. She would learn just by living.

"The new scheme works splendidly," Annie reported to Mrs. Hopkins several days later. "Helen knows the meaning of more than a hundred words now, and learns new ones daily without the slightest suspicion she is performing a most difficult feat. She learns because she can't help it, just as a bird learns to fly." (Annie went on to tell how she had taught Helen the game of Hide-the-Thimble. That morning she'd hidden a cracker.) "She looked everywhere without success, and was evidently in despair when suddenly a thought struck her, and she came running to me and made me open my mouth wide. Finding no trace of it she pointed to my stomach and spelled 'Eat?' "

They fairly lived out of doors, a happy teacher and a delighted Helen, and the Keller plantation in the springtime—when everything was bursting into fragrant bloom, and every day saw new calves, chickens, and puppies arriving in the world—was a wonderful place for a little girl whose own mind and soul were just struggling to be born.

The child was astonished and thrilled when Annie let her hold an egg in her hand and feel the baby chick "chip-chipping" its way out.

And then there was the baby pig! Annie wondered what the dignified Mrs. Howe or Mrs. Hopkins—or indeed any of her Boston acquaintances—would think if they could see her trying to grasp a squealing, squirming baby pig while Helen felt it from nose to tail, and asked, "Did baby pig grow in egg? Where are many shells?"

One morning while she was writing her weekly "progress report" to Mrs. Hopkins, Helen came tearing upstairs into their room bursting with excitement and spelling "Dog—baby—" and holding up five fingers of one hand and sucking them. Annie's first startled idea was that one of the several Keller dogs had injured Mildred, but from Helen's delighted expression she knew that couldn't be the explanation. She could only follow her downstairs and across the lawn to the pump house, where in one corner Helen excitedly knelt beside one of the setters and her five newborn puppies!

"Baby—baby—mother dog," Helen repeated over and over.

Annie drew the child's hand over one and spelled "puppy," and Helen screamed with glee as the tiny things wiggled to get back to their mother. "Baby eat large!"

Her exploring fingers discovered the fact that the puppies' eyes were closed. "Eyes shut—sleep no." She pointed to each puppy, then held up the fingers of one hand. Annie spelled the word "five." It was obvious that she was thinking about something, then she lifted one finger, and said "baby." Annie guessed she was thinking about her sister Mildred. She spelled, "One baby and five puppies."

Helen nodded. After she had played with the puppies she asked for their names.

"Ask your father," suggested Annie.

"No—mother." Helen spelled decidedly. One of the puppies was definitely smaller than the others, and Helen commented, "Small—small—" frowning in effort to express exactly what she meant, and turning pleadingly to Annie.

"Very small," Annie supplied the word. Helen understood in a flash that "very" was the name of the new idea that had entered her head. On the way back to the house she took short steps, saying, "Walk small," and then mincing ones—"very small." Finding Mildred she remarked, "Baby small. Puppy very small."

The spring weather had been glorious, and Annie and her charge wandered over the countryside, usually to Keller's Landing, a wharf which had been much used during the Civil War but was now overgrown with moss and weeds. Annie showed the child plants, flowers and trees, told her about the Tennessee River, even caught butterflies for her. "I feel as if I never really saw anything before," she said. When they returned from these excursions Helen was always eager to tell her mother everything they had done, which delighted Annie. It was a painless and happy way of developing her mind and stretching the wings of her imagination.

As a matter of fact Helen was eager to "talk" to everybody, wherever she went. Once she was restored to her "human heritage of language and thoughts," as she herself put it later, and her rages were vanquished, she became a friendly, joyous little soul, ready to love everyone she touched, and anxious to teach others her finger-talk.

Even learning to read was an adventure. By the middle of May Annie was taking Helen up to a seat in a tree near the Keller house and teaching her the raised alphabet. She tried the words in the embossed readers first, placing the child's fingers on separate words, but she was plainly puzzled. Then Annie found the embossed alphabet, and made her touch the raised "A" at the same time she spelled "A" into her hand. Helen caught that idea, and soon was moving her finger over the other raised letters

herself. She learned them all in one day. Then Annie
made her touch the word "cat" in the reader and
spelled it. Helen was enthralled. She asked for more
and more words. She was positively enchanted with
the reader. One night Annie discovered she had
taken it to bed with her, and when asked about it
the next day, she told Annie, "Book afraid—cry
much. Girl not afraid. Book sleep with girl."

These readers were not in Braille. Progressive
though he usually was, Dr. Howe had never approved of Braille. He had invented his own "Boston
Line Type," which was made of regular letters embossed, and for many years it was the only type
used in books printed and circulated by Perkins,
although a form of Braille had been devised by
William Bell Wait, Superintendent of the New York
School for the Blind. Just about the time Annie entered Perkins one of the blind teachers there who
had been seized with the inventive spirit produced
a Braille system of his own. He christened his
brain-child "American Braille," and Mr. Wait named
his invention "New York Point." Annie knew American Braille, but Braille readers hadn't been available, so she had been obliged to satisfy herself with
the primers in raised letters, even though they were
harder to learn to read.

But Helen was impatient with the readers because they didn't contain her name or the names of
the people she knew, or indeed all the words she
could use, so Annie sent a list of words to Mr.

Anagnos, and that kindly man had them printed on sheets of stiff paper which Annie and Mrs. Keller could cut into separate words, and when they pinned the name "Helen" on her dress, and arranged the words "is, on, the, chair," upon a chair, and stood Helen on it, or pinned the name "Mildred" on the baby, and placed the sentence "is in the crib," on that piece of furniture, the child was thrilled. And when Annie set up the sentence in a small frame she had for the purpose, Helen would sit and touch each word lovingly, spelling the sentences on her fingers as another child would have repeated them aloud, and always begging for "more words—more words."

Undaunted by the fact that Laura Bridgman was at Perkins fully a year before Dr. Howe thought she was ready for reading, and that it was considered a very difficult task to teach any deaf child to read, Annie concocted a plan. The ordinary "See the cat. The cat can run. See the cat run," was much too inane for Annie. Helen should have an actual story. She was a lively child, always in action, so the story must have very real action.

One day Annie captured a mouse and put it safely in a box. Then, having set up her story in the little frame, she gathered up a friendly cat and settled herself and Helen comfortably at a table. Very slowly she guided Helen's forefinger across the first words: "The—cat—is—on—the—box," and at the same time placed Helen's free hand on the cat curled on top of the box. The child gave a quick gasp of surprise, and her finger hurried to the next line, "A mouse is in the box. The cat can see the mouse." Indeed Helen could sense that. Quick interest flickered in her face. "The cat would like to eat the mouse." Actually she was familiar with only three words in the sentence—"cat, eat, mouse"—but Helen started in alarm and shook her head violently; but Annie gently compelled the little finger to move along the next line. "Do not let the cat get the mouse."

"No, no, no!" said Helen. She grabbed the surprised pussy from her perch and deposited her on the floor. Then she swiftly covered the box with her reading frame. Annie made her see there was more to the story. "The cat can have some milk and the mouse can have some milk." Would she grasp this happy ending? There were new words here, and purposely Annie hadn't stopped to spell them out. She watched closely as the tiny fingers lingered over the final embossed letters. And then Helen's face beamed and she turned to hug and kiss Teacher. Then she demanded, "Helen give cat milk mouse cake?"

That was a sequel which Annie had anticipated. Almost the first and still the most frequent words on Helen's fingers were "Helen give—" "Helen give candy" and "Helen give cake." Now in response to the eager question, Annie spelled out a quick agreement and produced the food.

After the refreshments had been served to the actors in the little story, and Helen had been assured several times over of the safety of the mouse, she flung herself upon Annie with the demand, "More words—much words!"

Laughing, Annie taught her the word "story." Helen accepted it readily, but her cry was still the same:

"More story—much more story."

CHAPTER · 8

The Glorious Race

LATE IN MAY the lovely Alabama spring in which Annie had reveled turned into scorchingly hot weather. Even the Southerners suffered. "Indeed," Annie told Mrs. Hopkins, "the Tophetic weather has reduced us all to a semiliquid state."

But they were all genuinely worried about Helen. From an energetic, robust little creature she suddenly became nervous and excitable and listless by day and restless by night.

On one unendurably hot day she removed all her clothing and "sat in her skin" by the window fingering one of her embossed readers. Eventually the sun shone in unmercifully. Helen promptly closed the window, but when that action wasn't effective, she sought Annie and spelled "Sun is bad boy. Sun must go to bed."

When Annie asked her to bring a glass of water, she shook her head sadly. "Legs very tired. Legs cry much."

The combination of her nervously eager finger-talk and her unnatural languor brought gloomy warnings from several of the Keller relatives and friends: "You are allowing that poor child to be overtaxed. Her brain is much too active. You should stop her thinking."

"The very people who thought she had no mind at all a few months ago," commented Annie caustically. "But so far nobody seems to have thought of chloroforming her. She begins to spell the minute she wakes up in the morning and continues all day long. If I refuse to talk to her she spells into her own hand, and apparently carries on the liveliest conversations with herself."

To keep the child quiet with a relaxing pastime, Annie gave her the Braille slate to play with. She had placed a sheet of the stiff paper under the slab of wood which was crossed by the movable metal bar pierced by its many openings. Giving Helen the stylus, she showed her how, when she inserted the point of the stylus in the various holes, the pressure would make humps appear on the other side of the paper. Helen nodded her understanding and settled down to make humps she could feel. Satisfied that at last she had hit upon an occupation that wouldn't "overtax" Helen's mind, Annie turned back to her own writing.

Half an hour later Helen was pulling at her sleeve. "Letter—post office—" she spelled, pointing to the Braille-dotted paper.

Annie stared at her. "Letter?" she repeated incredulously. How could the child have any notion as to what a letter really was? She had taken Helen to the post office, and had explained she was sending "letters to Mrs. Hopkins and blind girls," but that was all.

Helen nodded vigorously. "Letter—envelope. Post office."

"What did Helen say in letter?" she asked.

"Frank," spelled Helen, naming a relative who was away. "Much words. Puppy mother dog five. Baby cry. Hot. Helen walk—no. Strawberries very good. Frank come. Helen kiss Frank. Teacher put letter in—" she lacked the proper word, but she demonstrated her meaning by folding her "letter" and going through the pantomine of slipping it into an envelope and sealing it. "Now go post office?"

Annie was regarding her pupil with something very close to awe. Today was the second day of June—not quite two months since the "water" episode at the pump house had opened the door of Helen's mind. And now not only was she forming coherent, if incomplete, sentences by herself, but giving every evidence that her reasoning ability had

reached the stage where she understood perfectly
well what a letter was and what should be done
with it. Moreover she had mentally composed one
which would have been a very creditable produc-
tion for any child her age.

After she had succeeded in persuading Helen
that Nancy, her favorite rag doll, needed attention,
Annie turned back to her unfinished letter and
with racing pen proceeded to tell Mrs. Hopkin's
about Helen's "letter." Then she hesitated, about to
sign her name, and then impulsively wrote on:

And right here I want to say something for your ears
alone. Something within me tells me I shall succeed beyond my dreams. Were it not for the circumstances that
make such an idea highly improbable, even absurd, I
should think Helen's education would surpass in interest
and wonder Dr. Howe's achievement. I know she has
remarkable powers, and I believe I shall be able to de-
velop and mold them. I cannot tell how I know these
things. I had no idea a short time ago how to go to
work. I was working in the dark. But I know now, and
I know that I know.

Did this sound boastful? She didn't mean it so.
Annie bit her lip and was tempted to scratch it out.
Only the week before her letter had been a lament
about her inadequacy for her work, that her mind
was full of undisciplined ideas, skips and jumps and
dark corners, that she needed a teacher as much as
Helen did. But Mrs. Hopkins knew Annie. She

would realize this was not bragging, only a confidence between the two that now Annie felt that the path was opening before her, and that she was being guided in the way she was to go. Now she ended her letter:

Already people are taking an interest in Helen. She is no ordinary child, and people's interest in her education will be no ordinary interest. . . . I will write freely to you about everything on one condition. It is this: You must promise never to show my letters to anyone. My beautiful Helen shall not be transformed into a prodigy if I can help it.

When the weather continued too hot to roam outdoors, Annie decided to take advantage of Helen's delight in letters, and began teaching her to write. But she didn't begin with Braille. All her life Annie Sullivan would have the passionate conviction that the blind should not lead a segregated life. Helen was a blind child in the midst of seeing relatives and friends. "Talking" had to be carried on with the finger alphabet, reading must be in Braille or embossed print, but if Helen was to have a natural life and associate with normal people, as Annie was beginning to hope and dream she would, in the natural course of events she would come into contact with people who couldn't be expected to learn either her finger-speech or Braille, so she must have some avenue by which she could be understood by ordinary persons. The answer to that would be the square-letter, printlike script, written in pencil, that had been taught at Perkins.

Assembling the necessary materials, Annie remembered ruefully how stubbornly she had rebelled against the lessons in learning and practicing this writing in the days of her own blindness. None of the Perkins pupils enjoyed it—there is no pleasure in doing something one cannot examine and admire for oneself once it is done—but most of the blind learn it gladly for the pleasure of being able to write private letters. Annie had no correspondents and never expected to have friends who would welcome her letters, so in consequence she had made writing period a torture for both her teachers and herself.

Could she make it enjoyable, or at least painless, for Helen?

Calling the child to the little table she set up, she told her she was going to "show Helen how to write letters like Teacher." She placed the child's finger on the letter "C" printed in the print-script on an alphabet sheet in raised letters, at the same time making "C" with her fingers. Then she guided the little hand to the writing board with its grooved lines, and giving Helen the pencil, made her understand she was expected to repeat the "C" she had felt with the pencil between the grooved lines. Helen accepted it as a new game, and wiggled with delight. She learned seven of the square letters very quickly, and sat at the writing table for hours, feeling with her left forefinger to see that she was forming and spacing them properly, exactly as Annie had taught her to do. A few days later, with some help from Annie, she produced the sentence, "Cat does drink milk," and, flushed with achievement, carried it to her mother to be spelled out.

At sight of the intelligent, readable words written by the child who had been so locked in hopelessness a few weeks before Mrs. Keller's eyes brimmed over. Her emotion must have been carried into her fingers, because Helen's expression was both mystified and troubled. "Helen wrong? Mother does cry!"

On June 17 Helen was triumphantly writing her first letter to her cousin Anna, the words uncapitalized and strung together without punctuation, but unmistakably a letter.

helen write anna george will give helen apple simpson will shoot bird jack will give helen stick of candy doctor will give mildred medicine mother will make mildred new dress

Even when "a glorious thunder tempest" had broken the intense heat wave and Helen was her sturdy, active self again, her enthusiasm to "write letters like Teacher" increased. Perhaps she sensed that here was something that she could do like other people. She had been aware long before Annie came that she wasn't like the rest of her family and their friends. She was conscious they didn't make signs or "talk on fingers," or feel their way about. She had touched the letters Annie wrote to Mrs. Hopkins, and knew there were no humps to feel as there was with the "letters to blind girls." Perhaps she understood that the pencil writing was a link between her and seeing, hearing people. And Helen had a great advantage over the children at Perkins. Writing was never a set "lesson" for her—something she was required to do at a certain time regardless of whether she wanted to do it or not. For her it was sheer entertainment. Perhaps that is the secret of Helen Keller's outstanding achievements—that for the first two years of her education she didn't realize she was being "educated." She had Teacher's undivided attention, and Teacher had the imagination and the wit to be reckless with rules and routine. Learning never was a stint or a chore for little Helen Keller—it was fun and adventure.

When she and Teacher climbed a tree and she handled the blossoms or the leaves, when she held a flower while Teacher talked about it, or fed her pet rabbits and pigeons, or with pebbles built dams on the bank of the Tennessee River, or read the tidbits of stories Annie made up for her in the reading frame, she knew she and Teacher were having a wonderful time, but she couldn't know it was the beginning of a race that was to keep Annie breathless for a good many years—the glorious race of teaching Helen all the things she needed and wanted to know.

And there never was an end to what she wanted to know. One day her doctor uncle, James Keller, sent her a letter inviting her to visit him in Hot Springs. Helen was thrilled with the letter as well as the invitation, but she was fascinated by the name Hot Springs, and Annie's somewhat limited knowledge of hot springs was strained almost to the breaking point.

Helen was acquainted with springs—there were several around Tuscumbia; indeed, "Tuscumbia" was the Indian word for "Great Spring"—but she was astonished to know hot water could come up out of the ground.

"Who made fire under the ground? Is it like fire in stove?"

Annie racked her brains for the little she knew of geology, and her answer that some stones very deep down in the earth were hot like Cook's stove did seem feeble.

"Does hot water burn roots of plants and trees?" Helen demanded next. Annie assured her that it didn't.

"Why?"

Question after question, but finally she could

think no more, and Annie sighed with relief when Helen trotted out to the wide hall where her mother sat sewing, and proceeded to "read" the letter to her. She knew it by heart, and held the paper solemnly before her own eyes, just as Annie had done, and spelled off each sentence. After her mother had hugged and praised her, she spelled "Read letter to Mildred," and hurried to find her baby sister. On her way she encountered the setter, Belle, and dragged her along. She found Mildred on the floor, and sat down herself, while the amused Annie and Mrs. Keller watched from the doorway. Helen looked very serious as she began to read, but she frowned as she felt Belle yawn, and when Mildred tried to take the letter she pushed her away. Then Belle got stealthily to her feet, and tried moving away, but Helen caught her by the neck and made her lie down. Then she felt for the letter. It was gone! Probably she suspected Mildred, for she made the little sound that was her "baby call." Then she stood very still as if trying to catch the vibrations of the tiny feet. Having located them she went straight to the little culprit and discovered her chewing the precious letter. This was the final straw Helen snatched the letter and slapped the baby hands soundly. Annie and Kate Keller flew to the rescue. When the baby's wails had subsided, Annie drew Helen to her and asked "What did you do to baby?"

Helen looked worried, hesitated, and then said, "Wrong girl did eat letter. Helen did slap very wrong girl."

Annie kissed her. "But Mildred is very small, and she really did not know it was wrong to put Helen's letter in her mouth."

"I did tell baby no, no, much times!" expostulated Helen.

"Mildred does not understand your fingers, and we must be very gentle with her."

Helen shook her head. "Baby not think. Helen will give baby pretty letter." She turned from Annie, and ran upstairs. In a few minutes she was back with a sheet of neatly folded paper on which Annie could see she'd written a few words. Putting it into Mildred's chubby hands, she spelled to her mother, "Now baby can eat all words!"

It was odd how interested she was in things she couldn't know by touch, like the writing in the letter. When they went on walks or for rides she was always demanding "What does Teacher see?" Coming home from a visit to her grandmother in Huntsville, the thing that seemed to have impressed her most vividly was a ride to the top of a mountain. Annie had told her, "The clouds touch the mountains softly, like beautiful flowers." When Helen was describing the ride to her mother, she asked her if she would "like to see very high mountain and beautiful cloud caps?" And she became passionately interested in color. She found the word "brown" in one of her readers one day, and of course asked what it meant. Annie tried to explain, and added that her hair was brown, and Helen immediately wanted to know, "Is brown very pretty?"

After that she had to make a tour of the house and learn the color of everything she touched! When Annie told her Mildred's eyes were blue, she said, "Are they like wee skies?"

Once she had finished touching everything she could reach in the house, she was ready to go outside to the barns and the hen houses, but Annie collapsed into the hammock.

"Teacher is very tired," she explained. "Helen must wait until another day to go to the barns."

The child was penitent. She dropped down beside Annie cheerfully enough, but even so there was no respite.

"What color is think?" was one of the restful questions she shot at Annie.

By the end of July Annie began teaching Helen to write in Braille, and the child was delighted, once she grasped the idea that now she could read what she wrote for herself. Now Helen had mastered four alphabets: finger, the square-hand pencil print-script, embossed, and Braille. Of them all, writing Braille is the most difficult, since it must be written right to left, reversing the order of the letters, in order that the Braille humps may appear in correct order when the page is turned over to be read, all of which was no mean achievement for a child who had just passed her seventh birthday. She would soon have to learn Braille arithmetic as well.

But it was far from all work, even for Annie. In November they took Helen to the circus, and as Annie remarked, they all had the time of their lives. The circus people were delighted to have Helen present, and were very generous in granting permission for her to go everywhere it was safe to go. She fed the elephants, and was allowed to climb on the back of the largest one and sit on the lap of the "Oriental Princess" while the great beast marched around the ring. She handled some lion cubs, and told the keeper, "I will take baby lions home and teach them to be mild." She shook the paw of a huge black bear, and was delighted with the monkeys. Annie wrote:

One cute little fellow stole her hair ribbon, and another tried to snatch the flowers out of her hat. I don't know who had the best time, the monkeys, Helen or the spectators.

One of the leopards licked her hands, and the man in charge of giraffes lifted her so that she could touch their long necks. She also felt the Greek chariot, and the driver wanted to take her around the ring, but she "was afraid of many swift horses."

All the riders and clowns and rope-walkers let her feel their costumes and Helen kissed them all.

But the high spot of that first year for both Annie and the Kellers was Christmas, the first Christmas in her seven years of which Helen was truly aware. Oh, there had been other years when she had realized there was something exciting in the air— she and Martha Washington had been set to work to help with the fruit and nuts for the great fruit cake, and had been allowed to scrape the various bowls—but it had been a matter of enticing smells and pleasant tastes. This now—this was the most mysterious, absorbing, wonder-filled sensation she had ever known.

The very atmosphere around her was vibrant with excitement and anticipation, and the child tingled with the enchantment of it. The family would enthrall her with half-spelled sentences which they pretended to break off just at the right moment, and for weeks Annie and Helen had been talking about Christmas, and all Annie's stories had been woven around it—not that Helen understood all the new and strange talk about Christmas, and Annie didn't bother to explain in detail; that was part of the Christmas magic.

When the Tuscumbia school children had their Christmas party Helen was invited, and Annie took her, always convinced that the child should be with normal children as much as possible. Several of the girls had learned to talk with her, and one little chap her own age spelled his name.

The tree was the first Christmas tree Helen had ever encountered and it puzzled her. "Who made tree grow in house? Who put many things on tree? Why?" She disapproved of the ornaments and packages and started to remove them, but Annie assured her it was a very pretty tree, and the packages were Christmas presents for everyone. One of the teachers suggested that Helen be permitted to hand out the gifts, and when Annie explained the offer, Helen danced up and down with glee. There were several packages for her, but she placed them on a chair, refusing to open them until all the gifts had been distributed. One child had fewer gifts than the others, and Helen insisted on sharing her own.

Helen was in such an ecstasy that it was difficult to tear her away from the tree and the children when the party was breaking up. It had begun at nine in the morning, and lasted until one in the afternoon. Annie was exhausted, and went home with head, eyes and fingers aching, but Helen was as fresh as a daisy.

Christmas Eve bedtime found her quivering with anticipation. Annie tried to warn her that Santa Claus did not come to even good little girls if they stayed awake too long and got up two or three times during the night to see if anything had happened to their stockings (Helen had hung two for good measure). Whereupon Helen promptly squeezed her eyes shut and retorted, "He will think girl is asleep!"

And then it was Christmas morning, and a little figure was feeling its way from room to room, rousing each member of the family and spelling out her first "Merry Christmas! Merry Christmas!"

Running to the fireplace she grasped both stockings—and gasped with delight when she discovered both of them were full. She danced about, beaming with joy, until a sobering thought struck her, and she came to ask Annie, "Did Santa Claus think two girls live here? Did he make mistake? Will he come and take presents away when he finds out?"

"No, no," Annie laughed. "Santa Claus knows all about you. These are just for Helen Keller!"

Not only were the stockings stuffed, but there were surprises on the floor, on the table, even on the window sill. Helen's eager hands discovered a doll's trunk with many new clothes for Nancy, and she observed, "Now Nancy will go to party." Finding a Braille slate that would be all her own, she hugged herself. "I will write many letters and thank Santa Claus very much."

In the toe of one stocking was the gold ring she had especially wanted. "Mrs. Hopkins gave that to Santa Claus to bring to you," Annie told her.

"I do love Mrs. Hopkins!" Helen answered enthusiastically.

Indeed the child could barely move without stumbling upon a fresh surprise in dainty paper and ribbon, but when Annie finally brought forth her own gift last of all, a canary in a cage, the child really went into a rapture.

"If you are very gentle when you feed him, he will love you by and by and sit on your shoulder or your finger."

"And I will teach him much things." Helen touched the cage gently.

The Keller house was beginning to be pervaded by the fragrance of Southern holiday cooking, and lavish decorations made it a festive place. But Annie could guess, from the way both Captain and Mrs. Keller were watching Helen, that they must be having poignant memories of other Christmases when she had sat stolid and unheeding through all the gaiety, and that today her joyous face was the loveliest gift they had ever had.

Almost as if some unspoken message had passed between them, Kate Keller caught her eye, turned and said something impulsively to her husband, and then together they came to where she was sitting with Helen. "Miss Annie," Helen's mother said softly, "I thank God every day of my life for sending you to us, but I never realized until this morning what a blessing you have been to us."

Helen's father took her hand, but as was usual with him in times of emotion, he could only shake his head wordlessly, and only his strong handclasp and his eyes spoke for him.

CHAPTER · 9

"I Think!"

IT IS NOT RECORDED just when or why Annie's decision was made to take Helen and return to Perkins, but the idea must have begun crystallizing in her mind very soon after Helen's breath-taking response to her teaching became evident. Perhaps Annie's impetuous, impatient Irish-New England soul simply couldn't acclimate itself to the traditionally lackadaisical Southern methods. It certainly was a fact that Helen was so excited about discovering everything in her newly-found world that Annie's small supply of teaching materials was inadequate almost before she started. She needed books for herself, she needed embossed and Braille books for Helen, she needed them all in a hurry, and the South could not provide them.

Mr. Anagnos stood ready to send her whatever she wanted, but that kindly man, generous and willing though he was, could hardly dispatch all the books and special equipment at Perkins to Tuscumbia for the use of one lone little blind girl!

There probably were other arguments that kept rising in Annie's mind: In the school where Laura Bridgman lived Helen would have the fellowship of children who "talked" her own special finger-language. And every device used for teaching a blind child would be at her finger tips. Even if they stayed only a few months, and Helen was never registered as a regular pupil, she would have experiences and opportunities at Perkins that she couldn't have anywhere else. Perhaps Annie also gave a fleeting thought to the fact that in South Boston she would be near Dr. Bradford who understood her own eye condition and how to treat it. The hot glare of the summer sun on the red Alabama soil, and her constant following of Helen's increasingly rapid finger-talk were a greater punishment for her eyes than Annie would ever acknowledge.

Whatever her reasons, Annie's hopes and dreams of Boston, and her stories of the wonders of Perkins must have spilled out in her talks to Helen, for as early as September, 1887, Helen was writing eagerly, in a firm square-hand pencil script, to her unknown friends at Perkins:

Helen and teacher will come to see little blind girls Helen and teacher will go in steam cars to boston Helen and blind girls will have fun blind girls can talk on fingers Helen will see Mr anagnos Mr anagnos will love and kiss Helen

"Mr. anagnos" was glowingly enthusiastic over Annie's success and the progress of her pupil. He begged her to write an account of Helen's education for the Perkins Annual Report of 1887. Annie demurred. She protested she had nothing valuable to say. Actually, she was pouring forth such a terrific amount of physical and mental energy into helping Helen change from the groping, half-savage phantom she had found in March to the intelligent, winsome, happy child Helen had become by September, that she felt she had neither time nor eyesight to spend writing a review of things past.

Captain Keller, however, did not agree with her. Besides being Helen's proud father, he was a newspaper editor, and he could see the truly great story that was blossoming before his eyes.

"My dear Miss Annie, I agree with your Mr. Anagnos. I think it is your duty to give others the benefit of your experience. Helen's wonderful deliverance might be a boon to other afflicted children."

Annie surrendered reluctantly, but the report gave her a hard time, and Helen was puzzled by the many sheets of torn and crumpled paper scattered around Teacher's chair that day.

"When I sit down to write, my thoughts freeze,

and when I get them down on paper they look like wooden soldiers all in a row," Annie complained ruefully, "and if a live one happens long, I put *him* into a strait jacket!"

The Perkins Report was published in January with Annie's account, which wasn't in the least "wooden," complete with a grim photograph—to quote Mr. Anagnos—"of darling Helen and her illustrious teacher," in which the twenty-one-year-old Annie looks like a prim matron of forty, and the ordinarily radiant Helen seems a sour-looking, stolid child.

But Captain Keller had been right. This was a great story. The portion of the Report about Helen was reprinted and reviewed and quoted in nearly every newspaper and magazine. It captured the imagination of people all over America and England. They took the little girl in Alabama to their hearts. And it was no nine-day wonder. From then on, Helen Keller was news.

Meanwhile, quite unconscious of the fact that anyone outside of her family and the people at Perkins had ever heard of her, Helen was joyously learning how to be a natural little girl. And she could be normally naughty. Annie had a hard time curing her of pinching her grandmother. Once, when she was left alone to practice her writing, she smelled freshly iced coconut cake, and followed the enticing aroma to a sideboard in the dining-room where a tray of tiny cakes had been set out for expected guests. She was back at her writing-board, feeling well-satisfied and with the luscious taste still in her mouth, when a whirlwind descended upon her and Annie slapped the thieving hands soundly.

One day when she was supposed to write to a certain uncle she took it into her head not to use a pencil. "I will write Uncle Frank Braille letter," she informed Annie.

"But Uncle Frank doesn't know Braille," objected Annie.

"I will teach him," said Helen firmly. Annie tried to explain that Uncle Frank was too old to learn Braille.

"I think Uncle Frank is too old to read very small letters anyway," Helen flashed back.

Finally Annie succeeded in persuading her to take pity on Uncle Frank, and she produced a very brief letter, breaking her pencil six times in the process!

"You are a very naughty girl," Annie told her when Helen brought her the pencil the sixth time, but Helen shook her head gently. "No," she spelled, "pencil very weak!"

But the episode which really reduced both Annie and Kate Keller to the point of hysterics was the day Helen knew she was to be taken for a ride and decided to "dress up" for the occasion. She found her best dress, wet her long hair well, went in search of her father's hair oil, evidently decided to anoint her face as well as her head, and finished off with a generous application of powder. Then she proudly presented herself to her mother and gleefully announced she was all ready for the ride! Kate and Annie took one startled look at the bedaubed little figure, and then clutched at each other and laughed until they were weak.

In March Mr. Anagnos, returning from Florida, visited the Kellers and promptly did what Annie had passionately hoped he would—invited Mrs. Keller to bring Annie and Helen to Perkins for a visit later in the spring. He was the first important visitor Helen Keller had ever had. Other people had been amazed and awed by the child, but Mr. Anagnos was the head of a famous school for the blind. He *knew* the miracle which had taken place in one short year. Watching Annie, however, he was worried. Annie was too intense. She was literally pouring her life into Helen. Back at Perkins he wrote her what must have been one of the most understanding and tender letters she ever received:

I feel considerable anxiety about your overworking yourself, and I beg of you most earnestly, yes, I command you not to do more than is absolutely necessary between now and the first of June . . . Remember that if you break down you cannot be of service either to

Helen or to yourself. We want you to come to us well
and sound. Now, pray give heed to this earnest, parental
admonition, for it comes directly from my heart.

The Kellers decided that May would be a good
time to accept his invitation, and Annie eagerly began preparations. Until then she hadn't dared to
confess, even to her own heart, just how homesick
she'd been. But to go back to Boston—to see familiar
faces like Miss Mary Moore's and Mr. Anagnos', and
be with dear Mrs. Hopkins again . . . There had
been no opportunity to make friends here in Tuscumbia, and if there had been—Annie shrugged—
possibly there would have been no friends to make.
Southern chivalry was a peculiar thing. Everyone
was kind and courteous to her, but it ended there.
Kate Keller was her friend and a real love had
sprung up between them, but there was a chasm between every other Southern aristocrat and the Irish
working girl. Indeed, one Southerner had remarked
in Annie's presence that he would sooner die than
see his daughters earning their own living.

Helen came into the room the day Annie began
to pack. Her face was aglow with excitement, and
when she discovered Annie in the process of empty-
ing her bureau drawers she danced up and down.
"Teacher get clothes and everything ready to put
in trunk for Boston?"

"Yes!" said Annie, hugging her ecstatically.

"Mother is making me pretty new dresses to wear in Boston," the little fingers were spelling excitedly, "and I will look lovely to see Mr. Anagnos and little blind girls! Teacher will curl my hair beautiful, and I and little blind girls will have fun. I and little blind girls will go to school!"

"I and little blind girls will go to school!" That was a frequent phrase on Helen's fingers and in her letters, and it pricked Annie's heart. Joyous as the child was, did she instinctively miss the companionship of her contemporaries and the school life that is the normal pattern, without knowing she was missing something?

Helen was skipping lightly around the room, her flying fingers repeating to herself, "Boston! Boston! Boston!"

Watching her, Annie repeated the name under her breath. "Boston! Boston!" To Helen it was the password to Wonderland, to Annie it was the nearest thing to home that she knew.

Once settled on the train north, Annie drew a deep breath and felt a great feeling of sheer content stealing over her. Catching Mrs. Keller's eye she laughed a little. "I was just remembering my other train trip," she confessed, "coming down to Tuscumbia. My train ticket was such a snarled up affair I had to change trains at almost every stop. The agent who sold that ticket should have been hanged. And after Baltimore I was so uncomfort-

able in my thick woolens, and my eyes were bothering me and I kept wondering about Helen, if she
would be—if I could——"

Quick understanding filled Mrs. Keller's face. She
leaned forward and touched Annie's knee with a
gloved hand. "I know. Oh, indeed I know. I, too,
took a fateful journey, remember, when Captain
and I took Helen to Dr. Chisholm in Baltimore? And
then on to Dr. Bell—" the tears were very near; her
voice faltered, and this time it was Annie who
reached out an impulsively understanding hand.
"The day he saw us—and—and said Helen was a
fine, intelligent child and could be taught—that was
the first encouragement we'd had since Helen was
ill. And that's why we're going to stop at Washington now. I want him to see what's happened to
Helen—and I want him to see the miracle worker—
you, Miss Annie.

Fortunately for Annie, Helen plucked at her
sleeve just then. Even for Helen this was a different,
more joyous journey. Two years before she had
been a wandering, restless, uncomprehending little
being, requiring the attention of everyone; now,
with the questing spirit which has always filled her,
Helen loved every minute of the trip: the rolling
motion of the wheels, the strange, exciting smells,
the Negroes who came through the cars selling
tempting candy and popcorn balls, the attention of
the other passengers, and her mother's and Annie's

ever-ready descriptions of what they saw from the car windows. Neither Annie Sullivan nor Kate Keller could have guessed that the child was destined to travel to all parts of the world in the years to come, but even on this first trip she had the joyous readiness for everything that makes a born traveler.

And the trio did have quite an itinerary. Helen's uncle, Dr. James Keller, had told Captain Keller of a large medical convention which he was going to attend in Cincinnati. It was barely possible that some one of the famous specialists there would be able to help either the child's ears or eyes. By this time her parents knew in their hearts that sight and hearing were denied Helen, but Mrs. Keller consented to join her brother-in-law and have the satisfaction of knowing that every possible chance had been given the child. The doctors' tests proved that Helen would never know a gleam of light nor understand the meaning of sound, but no one could look at her joyous face, and hear her teacher or her mother translating her spirited remarks, and pronounce her "hopeless."

"There is something about her that attracts people," Annie commented. "I think it is her joyous interest in everything and everybody. Nobody pities her."

Indeed, one of the doctors remarked to Dr. Keller, "I would give everything I own in the world to have that little girl always near me."

"I Think!"

It was an amazed and amused Annie who found herself giving experienced and famous doctors information when they confessed themselves baffled as to how she had taught Helen abstract ideas like gladness, goodness, love.

"It seems strange that people should marvel at what is really so simple. Why, it's as easy to teach the name of an idea as to teach the name of an object. If you give a child something sweet, and he wags his tongue and smacks his lips, and hears the word *sweet*, or has it spelled into his hand, he will quickly adopt this sign for the sensation. Likewise, if you put a bit of lemon on his tongue, and he puckers up his lips and spits it out, and you label it *sour*, he adopts your symbol. But if you had called these sensations *black* and *white*, he would have adopted them just as readily. In the same way the child learns his feelings, and we name them for him—*good, bad, gentle, rough, happy, sad.* It isn't the word, but the capacity to experience the sensation that counts."

She hesitated, a little appalled at herself for her temerity in delivering such a lecture to these men, but the faces of the men gathered about her were actually respectful, attentive and absorbed. Annie had a flash of wonder. Here am I, little ignorant I, explaining to the wise men of the east and the west such simple things. She took a long breath and plunged on.

"Very soon after I came, Helen broke a doll of which she'd been very fond. She cried, and I said 'Teacher is sorry.' After a few experiences she associated the word with her sensation. When she did something well, or obeyed me, I said 'Teacher is happy,' and let her feel the smile on my face. She learned the word 'love' just the way any child would, by association."

They had a delightful week in Cincinnati, and Helen was sorry to leave, even to be on her way to the wonderful Boston.

Annie had been rather dreading the stopover in Washington. She had a shrinking sensation when she thought of meeting the famous Dr. Alexander Graham Bell, the man who was an inventor, a scientist and a teacher of the deaf. She was extremely conscious of her background, her crudeness, and every disadvantage she had ever had. Why had Mrs. Keller insisted on Annie's accompanying her and Helen to visit him?

She was sure she looked as awkward and cringing as she felt, but before they had been with Dr. Bell half an hour Annie was experiencing a feeling she had never known. The sense of inferiority that usually bedeviled her into carrying a chip on her shoulder was gone. Years later she said that Dr. Bell had a happy faculty of making others feel pleased with themselves.

Once again Helen sat on the knee of the man

who had been responsible for her escape from the "no-world" in which she'd been living when he saw her two years before. And once again the child was aware that this was someone who understood and cared for her. It wasn't only the toy elephant he gave her that day, but something about the man himself that made Helen adore him all her life. She was surprised and delighted to discover that he "could talk very fast on fingers," and Dr. Bell was astonished at her conversation and knowledge.

"Her achievement is without parallel in the education of the deaf," he said.

Coming from Dr. Bell this wasn't fulsome flattery. Dr. Bell came from a family which had taught the deaf for two generations. He knew. And when they left, Annie somehow knew she had a friend upon whose understanding and help she could rely.

Traveling had been delightful. They had enjoyed Cincinnati and Washington. But reaching Boston and Perkins—well, for Annie, Perkins spelled home, and for Helen it was like coming into her own. Here was Mrs. Hopkins, who had sent her the Christmas ring and was the housemother of the cottage where Teacher had lived when she was here, and who had been so good to Teacher. Here was Miss Mary Moore, the teacher Teacher loved. Here was kind Mr. Anagnos, who had invited Mother and Teacher and Helen to Perkins, and who sent her the books and stories she could read herself. He was so glad to see them! But most exciting of all, here were all the "little blind girls" she had been writing letters to all year. They were all crowding around her, hugging and kissing her, and *talking* to her—yes, they could all talk on their fingers! She had known about that before, of course, but it really hadn't seemed true. And it was wonderful! Up to now she'd had only Teacher and her mother to talk to. Oh, some of the rest of her family could "talk a little slow," but up to now she had been like a foreigner in a strange country who could talk to people only through an interpreter, but the blind girls could talk on their fingers almost as fast as she could. One thing did surprise her at first, curiously enough, and that was the fact that all the girls cupped their hands over hers as she spelled to them. Of course she knew they were blind just as she was, but somehow she'd had the idea that since they could hear, they also could see a little. It grieved Helen a little at first to discover that all of them lived in the dark as she did, but they were so happy and free that she soon forgot it.

Within a day all the "blind girls" had adopted her, and Helen was very much at home. They took her to their gymnasium and showed her how to play their games. They took her to their classes, and she was thrilled when she felt the raised maps and their many books. They showed her their beadwork, and how to model in clay. She loved the swings under the high grape arbors.

Annie took her to the great rotunda of the main building, and led her over the smooth stones, stopping to describe the soft colors and various designs of the mosaic floor, to the huge globe with its raised outlines of seas and countries, suspended in its solid wood frame. She explained the globe swiftly, and made Helen pass her hands lightly over it. Eagerness, wonderment and seriousness gathered in Helen's face as Annie made the globe revolve under her fingers. She stood quiet a minute, then she asked, "Who made the real earth?"

They went on to the exciting library. Helen nodded as her fingers identified the names of the stuffed animals and birds she knew, and she rapidly spelled their names and quickly learned many new ones. But what really lifted her to the peak of delight was the library itself. When she actually understood that here were dozens upon dozens of books either in raised type or in Braille, she hugged her mother and Annie in ecstasy, and then went around the room lovingly examining book after book and picking out words that she knew.

The visitors had arrived at Perkins May 29th, and Mr. Anagnos was in the throes of preparing his program of closing exercises, which wasn't too pleasant a task this year. Because of a reorganization of the Perkins classes there were no graduates, so there could be no commencement. Also, an outbreak of scarlet fever had shut down the kindergarten, and consequently the smallest children couldn't take their usual part in the closing day. However, resourceful Mr. Anagnos was planning a program of the usual addresses by famous men, music by the school band, and exhibitions of Braille reading and mental arithmetic by the Perkins pupils.

Then he had an inspiration. So many people had expressed interest and incredulity in the story of little Helen Keller. What was the child like? Was she actually as wonderful as the report had said? Well, here was Helen at Perkins. Why not let her take part in the closing exercises and answer for herself.

When he asked Mrs. Keller she consented readily enough, if Annie agreed, and Annie did. She hated the idea of Helen's becoming a "child wonder," but perhaps if she did take part in the exercises and people saw exactly what she could do it would spike exaggerated reports.

So two years after she had been a very quivering valedictorian for Perkins, Annie sat once more on the platform of Tremont Temple, this time with her already famous pupil beside her. As the fingers of Helen's left hand moved across the pages of the raised print, she spelled out the words into the air with her right hand, and Annie translated them for the audience. So rapid was the whole procedure that it seemed as though Annie was slowly reading aloud. One reporter commented that the story could almost be read from the changing expression in Helen's face, and that there was grace in every movement. The audience was enchanted.

Before Perkins closed for the summer Annie took Helen for a special visit with Laura Bridgman. Of all Annie's stories about Perkins, Helen's favorite was perhaps the tale of Laura Bridgman, who was so like Helen herself. Both had blue eyes and brown hair. Both had been terribly ill when they were small, and become blind and deaf. Helen had been six and a half when Teacher came, Laura had been the same age when Dr. Howe found her. Teacher knew Laura. Laura had taught Teacher how to spell with her fingers. She had even dressed the doll that Teacher brought to Helen from the "little blind girls." And always Teacher had promised to take her to see Laura Bridgman.

When the great day came Annie and Helen found Laura Bridgman sitting by the window in her room. She knew Annie instantly, and was delighted. When Annie drew Helen forward, Laura kissed her, but when Helen reached out inquiring hands to touch the lace she was crocheting, Laura jerked it back, spelling, "I am afraid your hands are not clean!"

Instinctively Helen wanted to "look at" Laura, but the woman drew back. She spelled to Annie, "You have not taught her to be very gentle!" and to Helen, "You must not be forward when calling on a lady!"

Rebuffed and a little bewildered, and probably with a strong desire to get out of Laura's way, Helen tried to sit on the floor, but Laura jerked the child up, and spelled emphatically, "You must not sit on the floor when you have on a clean dress. You will muss it. You must remember many things!"

Annie could see that the visit was obviously not a success. Helen was too much of a live wire for the sheltered woman. She said they must go. In her eagerness to kiss her hostess good-by and be off, Helen unfortunately stepped on Laura's toes, which displeased her greatly. Helen, in writing about this years later, said ruefully, "She made me feel like the bad little girl in the Sunday school books."

One of Kate Keller's favorite memories of this visit was the day she and Annie and several others were visiting Miss Moulton, the matron of Perkins. Miss Moulton showed them a gift she had received, a strange object which had them all puzzled until Helen felt it, hesitated, examined it again and then spelled "lemonade." She asked for a tumbler, put it in place, and the gadget was suddenly clear to everybody. It was a new type of lemon squeezer.

"How did you know, Helen?" her mother asked.

In answer Helen had touched her forehead and spelled twice, very emphatically "I—think!"

With the beginning of the summer vacation Mrs.

Keller decided to return south, leaving Helen and Annie to spend the summer in Brewster with motherly Mrs. Hopkins.

Annie had fascinated the child with her stories of the beach and the sea. Helen had known rivers and brooks and springs, but never the seashore, and the touch of the warm sand made her curl her bare toes gleefully. She had hard work standing still while Annie showed her how to put on her bathing suit, and then, holding Annie's hand, she ran down the beach and fairly danced into the water. The soft "slap-slap" of the waves against her ankles delighted her and she turned to laugh with Annie when she stumbled against a stone and fell forward into an incoming wave. It could have been only a minute before Annie's strong arms had managed to lift the terrified, struggling little body from the water back to the comforting warm and solid beach, but it was long enough to teach Helen that here was a force that could rob her of everything—air, strength, life—all at once. She clung to Annie's neck as if her hands would never let go. When they did, and she had recovered her breath and could think again, she demanded indignantly, "Who put salt in the water?"

It was several days before she could be persuaded that the ocean really could make a good plaything. For the first time in her life Helen Keller had met fear.

But Annie's gentle and wise coaxing did convince her that the ocean could be fun if one treated it with respect, and before the summer ended the seashore had become her favorite playground.

CHAPTER · 10

Into
Her Own
Country

HAPPY THOUGH BOTH ANNIE AND HELEN undeniably were at Perkins, it was becoming apparent that Helen was far from ready for the restrictions and regular routine of a school. She was growing too fast mentally and emotionally, as well as physically, to be caged in a classroom and pinned down to definite study of geography one hour and arithmetic the next. It simply didn't work.

Whether Annie had ever hoped or planned to stay on with Helen in the pleasant atmosphere of Perkins, where every teaching aid and skilled and sympathetic assistance would be at hand, she never said, but she did acknowledge the fact that Helen wasn't ready for normal school life.

123

"She's still like a child in a strange country where everything is new and perplexing," Annie confessed one day when she and Mrs. Hopkins and Fanny Marrett, one of the teachers in the Girls' Department, were gathered in Mrs. Hopkins' room. She glanced at Helen's absorbed little face as the child sat at the table, bent over her Braille slate, "She must gain sufficient language first of all—and that's always a mysterious and difficult undertaking for a deaf child."

"But she's learning very fast for all she's not in a schoolroom." Mrs. Hopkins assured her. "Remember the day we took her to Bunker Hill Monument? And how we'd no sooner finished descending the stairs when she announced there were two hundred and ninety-two steps—and she missed only two. And this morning"—here Mrs. Hopkins chuckled over the memory—"I happened to tell her that the soles of her shoes were very limber. She corrected me. 'Mrs. Hopkins is wrong. Soles are very flexible.'"

Miss Marrett laughed out. "It was comical to have her tell me, 'I am studying French and German and Latin and Greek.' And when I asked her to tell me something in French and Greek, bless you, she did! She said '*Se agapo* is Greek, and it means "I love thee." *J'ai une bonne petite soeur* is French, and it means "I have a good little sister." *Nous avons un bon pere et une bonne mere* means "We have a good father and a good mother." *Puer* is "boy" in

Latin, and *Mutter* is "mother" in German. I will teach Mildred many languages when I go home.' She seems to have an absolute craving for words. How did it all start?"

"She met a young lady in July who told her she was studying Latin in high school," Annie remembered. "Helen had to know what Latin was, and I told her it was a language people had spoken long ago, and spelled a few words for her. I told her *mensa* meant 'table,' *pater*, 'father'; *mater*, 'mother.' The next day she asked, 'Where is my *pater*?' Then she made friends with a German lady on the beach at Brewster, and she taught her the German and French words. And ever since we've been back from Brewster, and she discovered that Mr. Anagnos is Greek, she's been begging him to teach her Greek. And she remembers every word, even when he spells it only once."

"Like the outlandish name of Mr. Anagnos' Greek friend who was here in June," Mrs. Hopkins struck in eagerly. "You recall him, Fanny? Well, Helen met him just once, and when she saw Mr. Anagnos in September she asked him about Mr. Francis Demetrios Kalothakes."

"One thing does disturb me," Annie confessed. "I've made it my rule to use complete sentences, and yet she leaves out whole phrases in conversation. You must have noticed it. If I have something in my hand, she'll say 'What?' Or if I say I'm going upstairs, she'll ask 'To—?' or if I tell her I'm going for a walk she wants to know 'With—?'

"It's a funny habit," Mrs. Hopkins agreed, "but I wouldn't worry. Her mind is probably so full of questions she just doesn't have time to use all the words. But she will. You'll see."

Helen had slid from her chair, pushed the Braille slate and stiletto carefully aside, felt for the sheets she had carefully written, and then stood still, putting out a tentative hand, anxiety dawning in the expressive face. Annie had observed that she had not as acute or accurate a sense of distance and direction as many blind persons possess, and when it came to orienting herself in a strange place she was apt to be lost. Annie reached out a guiding hand, and at the familiar touch Helen's face became radiant. She came forward confidently, and Miss Marrett bent down to kiss her.

"Will you let us read what you wrote, dear?" she spelled into the child's hand. Helen nodded happily, and felt for the special little rocker Mrs. Hopkins had found for her. Once settled within easy reach of Annie's knee, she leaned forward, one hand in Annie's, almost in a listening attitude, asking once or twice, "You like? Mrs. Hopkins like?" as Fanny Marrett read the letter aloud. It was written to Mr. Morrison Heady, a poet who lived in Normandy, Kentucky, who had lost both sight and hearing as a young man, and who had become much interested in Helen through the Perkins report:

My dear uncle Morrie—I think you will be very glad to receive a letter from your dear little friend Helen. I am very happy to write to you because I think of you and love you. I read pretty stories in book you sent me about Charles and his boat and Arthur and his dream and Rosa and the sheep.

I have been in a large boat. It was like a ship. Mother and teacher and Mrs. Hopkins and Mr. Anagnos and Mr. Rodocanachi and many other friends went to Plymouth to see many old things. I will tell you story about Plymouth.

Many years ago there lived in England many good people, but the king and his friends were not kind and gentle and patient with good people because the king did not like to have the people disobey him. People did not like to go to church with the king. But they did like to build very nice little churches for themselves.

The king was very angry with the people and they were sorry and they said, we will go away to a strange country to live and leave very dear friends and naughty king. So they put all their things into big boxes and said Good-bye. I am sorry for them because they cried much. When they went to Holland they did not know anyone; and they could not know what the people were talking about because they did not know Dutch. But soon they learned some Dutch words: but they loved their own language, and they did not want little boys and girls to forget it and learn to talk funny Dutch. So they said We must go to a new country far away and make schools and houses and churches and make new cities. So they put all their things in boxes and said Good-bye to their new friends and sailed away in a large boat to find a new country. Poor people were not happy for their hearts were full of sad thoughts because they did not know much about America. I think little children must have been afraid of a great ocean for it is very strong and it makes a large boat rock and then the little children would fall down and hurt their heads. After they had been many weeks on the deep ocean where they could not see trees or flowers or grass, but just water and the beautiful sky, for ships could not sail quickly then because men did not know about engines and steam. One day a dear little baby-boy was born. His name was Peregrine White. I am very sorry that poor little Peregrine is dead now. Every day the people went upon deck to look out for land. One day there was a great shout on the ship for the people saw the land and they were full of joy because they had reached a new country safely. Little girls and boys jumped and clapped their hands. They were all glad when they stepped upon a huge rock. I did see the rock in Plymouth and a little ship like the Mayflower and the cradle that dear little Peregrine slept in and many old things that came in the Mayflower. Would you like to visit Plymouth sometime and see many old things.

Now I am very tired and I will rest.

With much love and many kisses, from your little friend,

Helen A. Keller

As the reading ceased the three women looked at one another and then at the flushed and eager face of the child before them with bewildered wonder. And then Helen was spelling again, anxiously, "Do you like?" And Annie caught her close. She was glad she did not have to speak. She could still spell, "It is the best letter you have written yet. Uncle Morrie will love it. How did you remember it all?"

"I think!" Helen touched her forehead in the familiar gesture.

"She certainly does think!" marveled Fanny Marrett, still gazing at her with awe. "How do you teach her such vivid history?"

Annie could only shake her head. She hadn't taught Helen history. On the way to Plymouth the day of the excursion she had given the child a brief story of the Pilgrims and their landing and now, three months later, she was pouring it out in a letter, supplemented by amazing human little touches provided by her own imagination.

Small wonder Mr. Anagnos exclaimed, "No other pupil in the school could have accomplished what she has in nineteen months."

As the days went on Annie admitted it was best for Helen to be taught alone, at least for the present. Her mind was still quivering with questions. If she were doing an arithmetic problem, for example, it might occur to her to ask how many steps there were to the stair landing—how many words were in her book. Another child might have been told, "Never mind that now. Just concentrate on how many apples are in the grocer's bag." But with Helen Keller postponement wasn't possible. Unsatisfied questions troubled her. Her mind was too quick and intent; not wayward, but, as Annie had put it, groping.

They were back in Alabama by November, and all through the winter and early spring they forged ahead, Helen gradually learning to follow a definite pattern of study and play until her days were well balanced and she was following a healthful routine. She had regular hours now for reading, writing, arithmetic, geography and language. And then in the spring the catastrophe that Annie had been trying to ward off as long as possible struck. Her eyes gave out. Years before, when she was in her teens, Dr. Bradford had warned her against overtaxing them, but how could she help it? The very act of watching Helen's fingers flashing out her thoughts at an incredible speed (she had been timed at the rate of eighty words a minute) must have been enough to make one actually dizzy. Of course added to this was the task of preparing the child's lessons and reading her increasing correspondence and all the books she both needed and yearned to "hear."

It was far from an easy thing to be the constant companion of a child to whom everything must be conveyed by finger talk. To Helen Keller it was as natural as normal speech. She says she is no more conscious of separate letters than one is conscious of them in reading. Nevertheless a good part of the time she had only to receive words into her palm— Annie had to spell them! It was exhausting work.

Laura Bridgman had been taught by special

teachers working in relays of a few months at a
time. Annie Sullivan was Helen's constant companion, teaching, traveling, playing with her, entertaining her by day, sleeping with her at night. It all
represented the most grueling punishment Annie's
eyes could have had, and when Annie's eyes rebelled she was always literally prostrated. The in-
human strain took its toll in April, 1889, and Captain Keller sent an anxious letter to Mr. Anagnos,
telling him Miss Annie's eyes were in a serious state,
and the doctor said she must have expert treatment
and a leave of absence for several months.

The letter found Mr. Anagnos wrestling with ill
health and pain of his own. He wrote Captain Keller that he deplored the dislocation of Annie's work
with Helen, that he had found a substitute for the
summer, a Miss Eva Ramsdell, who perhaps could
take over Annie's position permanently if necessary,
and who would arrive in Tuscumbia on May twentieth. He added that he was leaving Perkins in May
to go abroad for a year.

To Helen, Annie's going seemed like a confused,
troubled dream. But when the day came she made
a valiant effort and dashed away her tears "because
I mustn't grieve Teacher."

So Annie went back to Boston. It was the first
time she had been away from Helen for more than
a few days in the two years she had been with the
Kellers. It was the last time she and Helen would
be separated for many years. Happily for everyone,

131

Dr. Bradford worked another miracle and she was back in Tuscumbia by mid-September.

And Mr. Anagnos was not forgetting either Helen or Annie in the midst of his European journeys. He wrote Helen loving letters. Someone called them "small encyclopedias of travel." And on September ninth he wrote Captain Keller, urging him to allow Helen and her teacher to go to Perkins for the school year as special guests of the school.

Annie was gleeful when the captain accepted. Perkins certainly had much to offer both of them, and she knew that Helen had matured and steadied to the point where she could accept the school regimen.

As for Helen herself, she was beside herself with joy. She flung herself upon everyone spelling, "Perkins—Perkins—"

Watching her, Kate Keller choked and turned away. Yes, perhaps Perkins was the right world for a blind child, but Perkins and Boston were so far away from Tuscumbia.

Now for the first time Helen shared the lessons and the school experiences of other girls near her age, although Annie sat beside her, translating the teacher's spoken words. She supplemented the classroom teaching by answering all Helen's eager questions, letting as much conversation flow through the child's hand as the other girls heard with their ears.

Helen's school program sounds appalling. In November she sent her schedule to Mr. Anagnos.

Her school day began at eight in the morning, when she had an arithmetic lesson which she said she enjoyed greatly—although this early love did not survive very long. At nine she went to the gymnasium with the other girls. Ten o'clock found her studying geography, and she thought of Mr. Anagnos when she discovered Athens on the map. At eleven she had a lesson in "form," whatever that may have been; and at twelve she studied zoology. By two in the afternoon she was sewing, at three she went for a walk, and her reading and writing lessons came at four and five.

"The little student was fully occupied from morning until evening," commented Mr. Anagnos, "and she did not have much leisure for amusement."

One can see that.

Furthermore, the five o'clock reading, writing and talking Helen spoke of were being done in French!

"Will you teach me French?" Helen had asked Fanny Marrett one day as they sat together at the dinner table. Miss Marrett had a full teaching schedule on her hands, but looking into the eager face turned toward her she couldn't find the heart to refuse. She only ventured to remind Helen that the only free time either of them had was five o'clock in the afternoon. Helen seized upon the hour gleefully and it became a high point of the day for her. If she and Annie had strayed too far from Perkins on their afternoon walk, she would beg Annie to run part of the way home, or she would be very late for French! And five o'clock always found her in her little rocking chair, face turned expectantly toward the door, "listening" with her feet for Miss Marrett's footsteps.

Fanny Marrett began by giving her short sentences in English, phrases used in everyday conversation, and then repeating the same sentences in their French form. Helen would spell them over two or three times, first slowly, then rapidly, and then nod in quick satisfaction and ask for another sentence. Her teacher was a little awed at the rapidity with which the child learned. Each day she used all the sentences she had learned on the previous days, and even formed new sentences of her own with the words she knew. She like to write them in Braille. When she made mistakes she could laugh at herself: "I have been writing very funny French."

Miss Marrett copied a short story in Braille. Helen was delighted, and begged for more. She could read the stories easily, and even translate them into very readable English. And then one day she announced, "I am going to surprise my dear Mr. Anagnos. I am going to write him a letter in French, quite by myself."

Fanny Marrett and Annie watched the happy

child as she bent over her writing board, absorbed in carefully forming each letter in her firm, beautiful print-script, and then exchanged wondering, incredulous glances.

On the 18th of February, 1890, the letter followed Mr. Anagnos to his hotel room in Athens. He always opened Helen's letter with a real sense of anticipation. She had a definite talent for writing good letters and he had been genuinely proud to show her latest one to Queen Olga of Greece. But when he unfolded this new one he sat staring at it in stupefaction. In French! Not just a scattering of a few words or phrases as Helen had a habit of doing in her letters—this was completely in French, and entirely her own thoughts and work. And very good French it was, on the whole.

"No one can imagine how surprised and delighted I was." Mr. Anagnos wrote later. "With all my faith in her abilities I was not quite prepared to believe she would accomplish in three months what anyone else in America would require a year to do. Yet the proof was most convincing."

"I hope you will answer her in French," Annie had written. "That would delight her vain little heart."

But Helen herself was unconscious that she was accomplishing anything extraordinary. She responded to words the same way another child would to color or music. She loved words. Laura Bridgman, overwhelmed by the thought of thousands of words to master, had once cried out, "It makes my head ache to think of so many words." But to nine-year-old Helen Keller every new word was like a new door into the world that fascinated her.

CHAPTER · 11

"I —am— not—dumb—now!"

THE YEAR 1890 was full and important for both Helen and Annie. Blissful as Helen had been during her first visit to Perkins, she had been too undeveloped mentally to seize and hold the things Perkins had to give her. But now it was different. Now she was fairly breathless to investigate and absorb everything. School wasn't a routine to Helen; it was an adventure.

"Tell me more," she kept begging Annie. "I am curious about all things!"

She wrote a list of questions for Annie one day:

I wish to write about things I do not understand. Who made the earth and the seas and everything? What makes the sun hot? Where was I before I came to Mother? I know that plants grow from seeds, but I am sure people do not grow that way. I have never seen a child plant. Little birds and chickens come from eggs. I have seen them. What was the egg before it was an egg? Why does not the earth fall? Tell me something Father nature does. May I read a book called The Bible? Please tell your little pupil many things when you have much time.

A feeling of complete inadequacy swept over the twenty-three-year-old Annie. She quailed, but she followed her habit of satisfying Helen with as honest and intelligent answers as she was capable, and she made hurried excursions to the wisest books she could find, and answered the child as straightforwardly and simply as possible. Helen sat silent for a while, and then reached out to touch Annie's arm gravely. "What is my soul?"

Not an easy question for one who had no orthodox religious faith. Annie answered slowly and carefully, "No one knows what the soul is like, but we know it is not the body, and it is that part of us which thinks and loves and hopes, and which Christian people believe will live on after the body is dead. No one can see the soul. It is invisible."

Helen drew a long breath. It was a big thought for a child of ten, particularly for one to whom everything was invisible. Annie watched her face, and waited. She never forgot the gradual light that spread over Helen's face, nor her slowly-spelled words:

"But if I write what my soul thinks, then it will be visible, and my words will be its body!"

As the days went on Helen's interest in soul matters continued to build up. She had been taken to church occasionally, but no religious training had been tried, except by one relative in Tuscumbia, who had succeeded only in baffling the poor child by telling her that "Mr. God" had made her and everything out of dust, and was her loving father.

"And I know I am made out of flesh and bone," Helen reported to Annie, pinching herself, "and that my father is Arthur Keller. She must not make so many mistakes."

But that had been a year ago. Helen had met the names God and Heaven many times in books. She knew the meaning of death. She had to know more. When someone told her about the beauty and happiness in Heaven, she demanded, logically enough, "How do you know, if you have never been dead?"

Here was a problem Annie knew she wouldn't be justified in handling alone. She thought of the Right Reverend Phillips Brooks, who was a member of the Perkins Corporation. He had seen Helen and was interested in her, and Annie liked and respected Dr. Brooks. When she visited him to ask his help she liked him still more. She took Helen to his study, and the most distinguished clergyman in New England sat down with Helen Keller on his knee while Annie knelt beside him to interpret, and Helen spelled out her anxious questions:

"Who made God? Did you ever see Him? What is a spirit? Why does God think it wise to send people very great sorrow sometimes? I am blind and deaf and dumb and I cannot understand."

Holding the child close, Dean Brooks told her of God the Father, and the life of Jesus, His Son, in what Annie called the simplest and most beautiful words. They understood each other at once, even though they had to speak through Annie's fingers.

It was the first of several visits, and in between Helen wrote him letters, and Dr. Brooks always took pains to answer them in loving detail. How much Helen loved him was proved when, given the privilege of naming her baby brother, born a year later, she called him Phillips Brooks.

Dr. Brooks wasn't the only famous person Helen and Annie visited. One Sunday afternoon they were invited to call on Dr. Oliver Wendell Holmes. He enthroned Helen in his own big armchair, and delighted her with the many curios he brought her to examine. He asked her if she knew any of his poems, and she recited "The Chambered Nautilus." They saw him often after that.

They were also invited to visit John Greenleaf Whittier, and Helen asked him many questions about his poem, "In School Days." He was one person who thought Annie just as important as Helen. When Annie timidly asked for his autograph, he wrote:

With great admiration of thy noble work in releasing from bondage the mind of thy dear pupil, I am truly thy friend,

John G. Whittier.

And turning to Helen he said, "She is thy spiritual liberator."

He led Helen to the gate, kissed her, and asked her to come for another visit. But he died before she could visit him again.

Boston opened many famous and influential doors to Helen. Dr. Edward Everett Hale was proud to call her his cousin. She knew Julia Ward Howe and was a friend of Mrs. Howe's granddaughter, Rosalind Richards, and Boston's "Sugar King," John Spaulding, almost considered himself her godfather.

"Helen was petted and caressed enough to spoil an angel," Annie remarked, "but I don't think it is possible to spoil her. She is too unconscious of herself and too loving."

Boston certainly was both good for Helen Keller and good to her. In Boston she met so many normal people, and made friends with them so easily, that there never was any danger of Helen Keller's becoming the recluse Laura Bridgman was; and many of these friends were wealthy and influential enough to smooth her way when her father's rather shaky finances collapsed. Perhaps there were Bostonians who sent their first invitations out of curiosity because she was hailed as the eighth wonder of the world, but once they saw her the second invitation came for her own sake. She was so joyous, genuine, and utterly unaware that she was remarkable!

Perkins was good for her too. Annie wrote a grateful letter to Mr. Anagnos:

This year at the Institution has been invaluable to her. It has done more to enrich and broaden her life than many years of study at home would have done. (In the same letter she tells him—) In arithmetic, geography, zoology and botany she is keeping up with girls four and five years older than herself.

Perhaps the greatest gift Perkins gave Helen was the companionship of girls of her normal school age, who could talk to her without Annie's standing by as interpreter.

Helen threw herself joyously into all the doings of the school, from the games in the gymnasium and playgrounds and the weekly concerts—She loved the concerts. "Quick music makes my heart dance!" she said—to the recitations on Exhibition Days. She seemed to be at the peak of her happiness, and then Annie saw a change coming over the expressive face, a look of perplexity, wonderment, a vague sadness. She touched her lips and her throat frequently. Pain gripped Annie's own throat as she watched and waited. She could guess what was stirring in the child's mind, and wondered how she was to cope with it. And then came the question that tore at her heart: "How do the blind girls know what to say with their mouths?"

"Because they can hear," Annie said gently.

"Do deaf children ever learn to talk?"

Annie was too honest to give the comfort of a denial. She drew the child close and carefully explained. "Yes, they do, sometimes. There are schools where deaf children are taught to talk. But you see, they can see their teachers' lips, so they can learn to read what other people are saying, and then learn to make their own teeth and lips go the right way——"

"I can feel your mouth!" Helen was interrupting passionately. "I could learn—oh, Teacher, please teach me. I can talk now. I can say"—she ceased spelling, and pronounced the words slowly and explosively—"Mom-mom! Pup-pup! Ba-by! Siss-ter! Teach-er!"

She had indeed caught these few words from Annie's lips, and said them distinctly. Annie knew that Laura Bridgman had also expressed this instinctive longing to speak, and had learned several words. But this was something she honestly felt would be beyond the ability of even Helen, remarkable as she knew the child was. In this—what was there to be had except bitter failure?

And then something incredible happened. The door opened. Mrs. Hopkins was bringing in a vis-

itor, Mrs. Lamson, who had been one of Laura
Bridgman's teachers, and had just returned from
a tour through Sweden and Norway. Annie thought
she seemed unduly excited, and wondered about it.
She looked toward Mrs. Hopkins, but that good soul
had quietly left the room. Mrs. Lamson drew Helen
to her and began telling her about all the odd and
interesting things she had seen—the fjords, the mid-
night sun, the remains of a Viking ship—and then
suddenly she paused, drew a sharp breath, looked
searchingly into the vivid upturned little face, and
then her fingers began to tremble as she spelled,
"But Helen, the most wonderful thing I saw in Norway was a girl—a girl just like you, do you understand? Only she doesn't spell on her fingers at all.
She doesn't know a single letter of the finger alphabet! Her teacher taught her to know what people
say by touching his lips and throat. And she learned
to talk the same way—by feeling the vibrations the
words made in her own throat. I saw and talked
with her myself. Her name is Ragnhild Kaata."

Helen stood transfixed. All her pent-up longings
and hopes and doubts were flooding into her face.
Annie knew she wasn't conscious of another word
Mrs. Lamson said.

Looking at the radiance in her face, the tears
started in Mary Lamson's eyes; she caught Annie's
hand hurriedly, and then slipped away to leave
Annie to kneel before the trembling child. At her

144

touch Helen spelled joyously: "I am so delighted, for now I know I shall learn to speak too."

Annie swallowed. "If you will be patient a few days, I will take you to a kind lady who will know if it will be possible for you to learn to talk."

Helen laughed excitedly. "Oh, yes, I can learn! I know I can, because Ragnhild has learned to talk!"

Neither of them mentioned the subject again that day, but the child was flushed and excited, and did not sleep that night. And the next day she went about making various noises which Annie knew she considered words.

Knowing that the mechanism of the human vocal cords is extremely delicate, Annie sensed the need of immediate expert advice. The only person she thought would be qualified to give it was Miss Sarah Fuller, Principal of the Horace Mann School for the Deaf in Boston. Helen had been there once before, on her first visit to Perkins, but because everybody considered her blindness an absolute barrier to learning to lip-read or speak, nothing had been attempted in her case.

Now it was different. Miss Fuller was delighted with Helen's enthusiasm and ambition. Of course she would try to teach her to speak.

Standing Helen directly before her she made the child feel the position of her tongue, teeth, lips and throat as she repeated the sound of the "i" in "it" over and over again. Suddenly Helen's fingers flew to her own teeth and tongue, and from out the silent throat there came an "i" sound so nearly like Miss Fuller's that it seemed like an echo.

"Ah" came next. Helen caught that one too.

"Now we'll try some words," Miss Fuller spelled. "It—miss—kiss—see—me——"

And wonder of wonders, Helen produced them all, broken, hollow, but unmistakable words. And Annie knew she had never heard anything that thrilled her more than the breathy, blurred words which Helen was laboriously forcing her long-sleeping voice to produce.

Perhaps in all the history of triumph over obstacles there is no more poignant or triumphant picture than the one of this nine-and-a-half-year-old child as she stands before Sarah Fuller, pulsating with the intensity of her purpose, and forcing her voice to break its chains of silence. For the victory she won that day liberated not only her own tongue, but the tongues of all who must pass their days in darkness and silence. Deaf and blind they may be, but they need not be mute and separated from the world.

When Helen realized she had succeeded in pronouncing her first complete sentence. "It—iss—warm," she cried from the combination of the strain and joy. And a little later she was saying what would be her favorite sentence for several weeks: "I—am—not—dumb—now!"

Sarah Fuller gave her eleven lessons. And then Helen and Annie carried on by themselves. Unfortunately grave mistakes were made. Speech for the deaf was in the pioneer stage. Not even Sarah Fuller or Dr. Bell knew what every teacher of the deaf knows now—that vocal exercises should have been given to strengthen and flex the long-unused cords before any words were permitted. Helen plunged eagerly into attempting whole sentences as soon as she could utter sounds. It was a bitter mistake. Her voice has never become the natural and intelligible thing she has yearned and worked for so passionately. But—she speaks. And as she herself said later, "My semi-captive thoughts no longer tugged at the chain that my own hand-spelling imposed."

This was the hardest undertaking either Annie or Helen had ever faced. With many qualms as to her ability to accomplish it, Annie was trying to teach the child the knack of lip reading as well as articulation. She would place one of Helen's fingers against her nose, one on her lips, and the rest of the hand at the side of the throat for the lip reading process, and patiently repeat separate sounds and then entire words by the hour. And then to give her an idea of the proper position of the lips, tongue and teeth in forming words, she made the child examine her own mouth and throat, just as Sarah Fuller had done. It wasn't easy. It wasn't even pleasant. Some-

147

times Helen's sensitive fingers would probe so far down Teacher's throat that Annie would gasp and gag. Sometimes it seemed to both of them it was impossible for Helen to capture the right formation of her tongue or the correct vibration of a word. Annie would end the lesson in exhaustion. Helen would practice until she was so overwrought and despairing that she cried. Only two such valiant companions would have had the unadulterated courage to go on week after week.

One thing held Helen to her course: "My little sister will understand me now!"

And at the end of six weeks Annie could report to Mr. Anagnos, "She is 'talking with her mouth!'" It was broken, oddly accented, but to her teachers and close friends, perfectly understandable speech —which was something of a miracle, for she had achieved in six weeks what it usually took the average pupil at schools for the deaf a year to accomplish.

Her friends at Perkins were delighted, but the letters to Tuscumbia breathed no hint of the amazing venture. Both Helen and Annie were guarding their secret well. Helen's first speech lesson had been in March, and as the weeks went on she was torn between her intense desire to make herself as intelligible as possible before her family knew she was talking, and her impatience for the June vacation to arrive.

And then, in May, just as the school year was drawing to a close, Annie had her first tragic experience of what a cruel boomerang an entirely innocent and truthful remark can be. A reporter from the *Boston Journal* asked her for an interview about Helen and her studies at Perkins. Perhaps she talked too freely, possibly the reporter managed to give her words a different implication, but at any rate Annie was quoted as saying that, although Helen had been given all the advantages and privileges of the Perkins teaching and equipment, she was not a regular pupil of the school.

"I have the sole charge of her," Annie had said, "and my salary is paid by her father."

This was true enough, and Mr. Anagnos had said the same thing several times, but Michael Anagnos, son-in-law of Dr. Samuel Gridley Howe, and Director of Perkins, might say a thing and have it accepted, while Annie Sullivan, former charity pupil could not.

It must be admitted that Helen's and Annie's status at the school was a little out of the ordinary. They were there as "special guests" at Mr. Anagnos' invitation. No tuition was being paid for Helen, yet she had all the benefits of the other pupils without being subject to the school's rules and regulations. And of course she did excite more interest and attention than all the other pupils put together. All of this had begun to annoy certain of the Perkins' authorities. And when the *Journal's* interview appeared containing Annie's truthful but rather tactless remark, it caused a furor, antagonized the trustees and brought a storm of accusations upon her head.

She was accused of "biting the hand that had fed her," and claims were made that Helen was far more indebted to Perkins than she was to Annie. Annie was pointedly told that "Alabama would be a more fitting place for her peculiar brand of gratitude than Boston."

Shaken and distressed, Annie gathered herself together and wrote a contrite letter of apology to the trustees. She told them that she would be the first person in the world to acknowledge the great debt Helen owed to Perkins and, indebted as Helen was, Annie was much more so, for both the past and the present. That without the help and encouragement of Mr. Anagnos and her friends at Perkins her work with Helen would be impossible. She ended her letter with the plea: "I beg you that though you blame me for indiscretion, you will not blame me for ingratitude."

Then she sent a copy of "the miserable interview" and her letter to the trustees to Mr. Anagnos.

The trustees apparently were not in a forgiving mood. It had been planned to have Helen demonstrate her speaking ability at the Perkins commencement program, but at the last minute the trustees refused to allow it. Their published report of the commencement said suavely that "for economy of strength she was not called upon to do it."

It was a weary, troubled and unsure Annie who packed Helen's trunks and her own for the return south. Had her thoughtless sentence barred the doors of Perkins to Helen just when the child most needed the opportunities and culture Boston could give her?

Helen on the other hand was jubilant at the thought of leaving Perkins and going home to finally reveal her long-cherished secret. She found the southbound trains unbearably slow.

"Where are we?" she would demand each time the train halted. "How long will we stop here?"

She spent most of the time talking excitedly to the patient Annie, talking merely for the sake of improving her voice up to the last possible moment.

And then the train was jerking to a halt at the Tuscumbia platform, and Annie, looking out of the window, told Helen that her parents and Mildred were waiting for them. Helen's knees felt suddenly strange. With her moist hand clutching Teacher's, she somehow got down the car steps and felt herself snatched into her mother's arms. But she drew back. Trembling, she stood very tall, and then slowly, carefully, and as clearly as she could, she spoke in the blurred monotone which is her voice:

"Moth-er—I—am—not—dumb—now. Mil-dred—I love—you. Fath-er—"

And then all three Kellers were upon her. She

151

knew her mother was sobbing convulsively. Even her father was crying. Little Mildred had grabbed her hand and was kissing it ecstatically.

Helen Keller is the one person to describe that moment:

"It was as if Isaiah's propecy had been fulfilled in me. *The mountains and the hills shall break forth before you into singing, and all the trees of the fields shall clap their hands!*"

CHAPTER · 12

"City
Of
Kind Hearts"

THE KELLERS SEEMED TO BE LIVING through a miracle during the next weeks. Kate Keller hung on every syllable Helen uttered, and the Captain went about proudly repeating Annie's account of Helen's determination to speak, and Sarah Fuller's surprise and praise for the child's quick mastery of the very difficult feat.

As for Helen herself, when four-year-old Mildred came in obedience to her call, and entered into the "game" of talking into her sister's hand, and for the first time in their lives she understood what her baby sister was saying, there was a sudden glory in Helen's face so poignant that it made Annie turn away. But she knew she was repaid for the ceaseless hours she had spent talking into Helen's hand.

It seemed there was no higher peak the Kellers could reach. And then Helen frightened them all one day by having a fainting fit. She acknowledged that she "felt a very little sick," and she seemed tired and weak. The doctor's examination showed no special illness, and Annie agreed with the Kellers that it probably had been brought on by the quick change from Boston's more bracing climate to hot and humid Tuscumbia, and that the child would undoubtedly be better in the cool mountain air. Accordingly they went to the Keller's summer cottage, Fern Quarry, in the nearby mountains. The abandoned limestone quarry was filled with exquisite ferns, thriving on the moisture of three lively streams hurrying and tumbling through it. The mountains were covered with tall oaks and evergreens, hung with mistletoe and ivy, and persimmon trees whose fragrance filled Helen with delight. It was a good place for a tired little girl to be, and try to forget for a while how hard she had to work to accomplish what other people simply take for granted.

Annie was suddenly realizing with a pang that Helen *was* tired. She possessed such boundless energy and enthusiasm for everything she did that it was difficult to hold her back, and she had, apparently, as she herself said later "danced through her lessons," and it wasn't until her voice lessons began that she had faced an ordeal. They had been a strain, and when the tension of the school year was released, something in her simply had to let go.

All that summer Annie and the family tried to help the child relax. She played with Mildred and their little cousin Louise Adams, explored Fern Quarry, and rode her donkey, Neddy.

One thing that especially pleased her during that summer was a letter from Laura E. Richards, Dr. Howe's daughter and mother of her friend, Rosy Richards, telling her that a lumber company in Gardiner, Maine, had named their new vessel the *Helen Keller.*

Sometime during the summer or early fall, Mr. Anagnos sent another generous invitation for Annie and Helen to come back to Perkins. This time Annie wasn't sure if it was the right thing to do. She wrote of her doubts. Helen might be welcomed, but Annie Sullivan——?

Mr. Anagnos brushed aside her reluctance. They certainly were to come. But it was November before Helen seemed to be strong enough to undertake another year of regular school.

She was excited to be back at Perkins and in Mrs. Hopkins' cottage, and was overjoyed to find Mr. Anagnos in his old place in the Director's office. When she flung herself upon him her joy threatened to block her welcoming words in her throat.

"Teacher says I have grown so tall you won't know me!" she told, him, proudly "talking with her mouth." And when he gave her the watch he had brought her as a coming home gift, she was so overcome that she couldn't even spell.

Mr. Anagnos was delighted with her ability to speak, but he was shocked at the appearance of the child. He had expected her to grow tall,' but to have the rosy, healthily active child of two and a half years before turn into this white-faced, nervous girl—! Observing her for several days, he grew distressed and alarmed.

"Nervousness and excitability are apparent in all her movements and conversation," he declared. Did she sleep well? Was her appetite good? No? Mr. Anagnos looked a little grim. What had been happening? He didn't like what he found out, and exclaimed bluntly, "An undue pressure of work was put upon her, accompanied by an unwarranted stimulation to overexertion!"

Considering that the previous year Helen had been carrying seven or eight subjects from eight in the morning until five in the afternoon, had studied French on the side, and then flung herself into the exhausting work of learning to talk and lip-read, this seems to be no exaggeration.

But it seems not to have occurred to anyone that Helen had never known a set schedule or regular lessons until a few months before she came to Perkins. All her education had been informal, and most of it out-of-doors in a southern climate; and then she had made the sudden transition to Perkins in wintry Massachusetts where she followed a fixed indoor school schedule, a schedule which, as Mr. Anagnos had already observed, left her little or no time for play or rest.

It was small wonder the child paid the toll for this program! It was time for another kind of plan and, Mr. Anagnos set to work mapping out a schedule of alternating rest, play, and exercise, both in the gymnasium and out-of-doors. There were no lessons. She might read and write—he knew Helen well enough to understand that she would be absolutely miserable without her letter-writing or her beloved books—but that was all. Helen was bitterly disappointed. She wanted to join in everything the other girls did. But Mr. Anagnos was firm.

"Not until you are very strong again," he told her.

His program paid off. By January Helen was her old, buoyant, vigorous self again. And in saving Helen Keller's health, Mr. Anagnos did the world a service he could never have dreamed he was doing. He was a man possessed of two great aims: to establish a library in memory of Dr. Howe, and to found a kindergarten for blind babies in memory of his wife, Julia Howe Anagnos, whose very last words to him had been, "Take care of the little blind babies." He accomplished both purposes. His kindergarten for the blind was the first in the country, and the library that he started at Perkins is now considered the best Blindiana Library in the country. But in saving Helen Keller's health he did a third deed which ranks with the other two, for only a person of Helen Keller's wonderful vitality could have done the work for the blind that she has done all over the world.

Mr. Anagnos saw to it that both her studies and her exercise were varied. Who else would have thought of having a deaf-blind pupil taught music? Odd as it seems, the deaf like music. Helen always enjoyed it, catching the vibrations through the floor, or by placing her hand on a piano or violin. For two and a half months she studied piano with Miss Mary Riley to improve her sense of rhythm and feeling for vibration. She even learned to play a short piece, "Echo."

And Helen wrote to her father: "You would be amused if you could see me at nine o'clock each day, for at that hour we learn sloyd. We learn how to saw and plane and measure exactly with a rule." A very progressive school Perkins must have been under Michael Anagnos.

But the hours both Annie and Helen loved most of all were the hours they spent riding horseback in the crisp Boston weather. Helen had been surrounded by animals from babyhood, and loved them all, and Annie was genuinely thrilled when she was on a horse. But one day, riding under some low-hanging branches, Helen was almost thrown off. Frightened, Annie half-scolded her.

"However could I have gone home to your mother without you?"

Shaken though she was, the imp of humor that always lurked in the child flashed out. "You needn't have gone home without me!" she sobbed. "You could have tied the pieces in a bundle and taken me home to Mother that way."

But the thing that was absorbing and all-important to her this year was the fate of a tiny four-and-a-half-year-old boy in a hospital in Allegheny, Pennsylvania, Tommy Stringer. A Rev. J. H. Brown, of Pittsburgh, who had met Helen and Annie the year before, wrote Annie about him. He had been blinded and deafened by some illness, his mother had died, and his father either couldn't or wouldn't take care of him. No one else wanted to be burdened, so the only available place for the helpless mite was the almshouse. It all reminded Annie too much of another hapless child, and sick at heart she poured out the whole story to Helen.

Helen had never considered herself as handicapped or limited, but she still had a vivid memory of her groping days before Teacher came. This baby boy was like her, only in a far worse plight. She had had a home and a loving, watchful family, the most wonderful teacher anyone could possibly have, and generous friends. Baby Tom had nothing. Her response was instantaneous.

"We must bring him here—at once."

Unfortunately that was far easier said than done. Annie knew there could be several barriers in the way, and for perhaps the first time she had to give

Helen the sad lesson in economics—that it isn't always easy, or even possible, to give people what they need, no matter how distressing their condition may be. Helen had always been fortunate in being surrounded by a loving family and generous friends. Intelligent beyond her years though she was, money had meant comparatively little to her. It must have been hard for her to comprehend that the thing called "money" could stand between Tommy and Perkins. That just because of money Tommy might have to spend his whole life groping in the blank, unhappy world in which she had lived before Teacher came to Tuscumbia. She turned a sober, intent face toward Annie while she "listened" to the explanation Annie was spelling. Her forehead furrowed with her perplexity and fear.

"But Edith Thomas and Willie Elizabeth Robin are both here in the kindergarten," she told Annie. "And they are both like me, blind and deaf!"

"Yes, but both Edith and Willie have parents to pay for them," Annie said, more sadly than Helen could guess. "This is a school, you know, Helen, a special school—not just a home for blind children— and special schools cost a great deal of money. It takes much money to print the embossed and Braille books, and make the raised maps, and buy typewriters and the sloyd materials. And children like you require special teachers. Miss Markham is Edith's special teacher, you know, and Miss Thayer is Willie's. Your father pays my salary. But poor Tommy has no family to pay for him."

Helen's face was still serious, but the first crest-fallen, troubled look was gone. "Then we will raise the money," she informed Annie. And for the next few months her campaign for helpless little Tommy Stringer was always uppermost in her mind. She wrote to her correspondents about him, and talked to her friends, asking for contributions to her "Tommy Fund." She denied herself sodas, of which she was very fond, because Tommy must come to Perkins. The forlorn little waif could not have had two champions more qualified to fight his cause than Annie Sullivan who had known what it was to be an unwanted child abandoned to the desolate, hopeless life of an almshouse; and Helen Keller, who knew what it was like to be a "little Phantom in a No-World."

When the Perkins trustees heard of the case, they agreed to admit little Tommy Stringer. Indeed, Mr. William Endicott Jr. was open-minded and gener-ous-hearted enough to say to Mr. Anagnos, "Luckily, the number of these hapless children is very small, and, as there is nowhere in the country a place open to them, why do you not arrange to take care of them all?"

Both Teacher and Helen breathed easier after that, but there was still need of the "Tommy Fund" to provide for his special teacher.

And then in the midst of her campaign for Tommy, tragedy struck at Helen. The summer before, Mr. William Wade, of Hulton, Pennsylvania, one of the kindest friends Helen and Annie would ever have, had given Helen both the donkey, Neddy, and a dog. Mr. Wade believed that blind children should have large dogs for protection and companionship, and in order to be sure that Helen's dog was large enough, he had given her a mastiff. Helen loved her, as she has always loved the many dogs in her life. Lioness was intelligent and loyal, gentleness itself, but her very size was sufficient to frighten strangers, and of course she had to be left in Alabama when Helen returned to Perkins. One day she was brutally killed.

It was the first sorrow of its kind Helen had ever had, and in addition to her loss, the thought of the dog's suffering tortured her. She had always kept Mr. Wade posted on the health and doings of Neddy and Lioness, and now she wrote a simple, sorrowful letter to his children.

Mr. Wade sent the letter to *Forest and Stream*, where it was promptly published. Helen Keller had become such a household personality to the English-speaking world and was so deeply loved that the reaction was immediate and overwhelming. It was as though she belonged to everyone, and everyone was indignant at the deed and wanted to make up to the child for her loss.

"A shower of offers to provide her with another

canine friend," as Mr. Anagnos put it, came from the magazine's readers. They came from Canada and England as well as from Americans. And Helen was pleased. What child wouldn't have been? And then the thought struck her. The Tommy Fund! She didn't have to have another dog, but Tommy had to come to Perkins and be provided with a special teacher!

She wrote personal letters to all the generous people who wanted to give her a new mastiff. She thanked them. "I love great, faithful dogs like Lioness, but I love little boys and girls still more." And then her letters went on to tell them about little Tommy, for whom the light and pleasant sounds had gone out, and who had no gentle mother to lead him about, and whose father was too poor to pay for his education. Instead of buying another dog, would they help her to educate Tommy?

And so, at ten and a half, Helen Keller embarked upon what would prove to be her life work—work for the betterment of the blind—and on the sixth of April, 1891, a nurse brought little Tommy Stringer from the Allegheny General Hospital to Jamaica Plain, where the Perkins Kindergarten for the Blind was located. A special teacher wasn't available for the child as yet, so Annie and Helen went to Jamaica Plain to take charge of him.

Helen was jubilant. She danced about, and hung over him, happy and confident. But Annie was absolutely appalled. It would have been next to im-

163

possible, she thought, to find a more unprepossessing, pitiful specimen of little boyhood.

Even as a "little phantom" Helen had been active, self-reliant, responsive, overflowing with signs of intelligence; this poor little waif was "a mere lump of breathing clay." He had spent most of his life in the hospital where the busy nurses had found it easier to care for him if he remained in his crib. In consequence he could barely sit up, could not walk, or even eat properly. He had no signs to indicate that he wanted or understood anything, made no response to a friendly touch. The one glimmer of intelligence that Annie caught—if it was intelligence —was that when Tommy was placed on the floor he tried to creep backward. Maybe, she thought, he had discovered that bumping into unseen things backward hurt less than head-on! Added to all this was his disconcerting habit of peacefully sleeping through the day and becoming restless and troublesome at night.

Annie wondered as she worked over him whether help had come too late. Had he lain unloved so long that his intelligence had receded too far to be called back now that sympathetic and understanding hands were being held out to him? Or—most cruel thought of all—had the illness that took his sight and hearing also damaged his brain?

Even Helen, for all her exultation over having him at Perkins, was a little disturbed and distressed.

"I did not imagine he would be so small and help-less," she confessed, and then added staunchly, "but I love him all the more for his helplessness. And Teacher will be very gentle and patient with him, and soon his mind will escape its prison."

Patience, thought Annie wryly, wasn't one of her greatest assets! But she must have had a special genius for reaching such children as Helen and Tommy, for in the three weeks she had charge of "Baby Tom" he showed remarkable improvement. Annie had succeeded in teaching him to eat prop-erly and to walk a little, and he actually was be-coming a pretty little fellow with a dawning interest in the life around him. He was responding to affec-tion, and would stretch out dimpled hands to climb into any pair of friendly arms and cuddle down with a sigh of content.

Nevertheless Annie breathed a sigh of relief when Miss Bull arrived to take charge of the little fellow and she and Helen were free to return to their usual school routine at the main school in South Boston.

Back in Mrs. Hopkins' familiar cottage, Helen fell to writing letters to all the contributors to her "Tommy Fund." She covered sheet after sheet, and Annie discovered to her amazement that each one was an individual, newsy note about "Baby Tom" and his progress. In one she spoke of his helpless-ness. One mentioned his dimpled hands, in the next she told about his affectionate ways. She also wrote

165

to all the Boston newspapers, thanking them for all their help, and asking them to publish the list of contributors.

No wonder her fingers grew cramped and she developed calluses on her thumb! But the letters were not a chore. She was simply so overflowing with enthusiasm about Tommy that it had to spill over.

In one thing she was disappointed. She fairly seethed with impatience for the day when he would spell his first word, but Tommy showed no desire to have anything to do with finger talking. Indeed, he was far more slow in learning anything, even the use of his hands, than Helen or Perkins' two other deaf-blind pupils, Edith Thomas or Willie Elizabeth Robin, ever had been. Annie surmised there might be two very sound reasons for this slowness: The little chap was still a good two years younger than any of the girls had been when their education began; and where they had been allowed to explore as much of their little worlds as possible, poor Tommy had been practically a prisoner in his hospital crib, unloved and forsaken. No wonder his small mind lay dormant. Now he had to learn the simplest things first, by instinct, before language or anything else would reach him.

Helen nodded in thoughtful agreement at Annie's explanation. "I remember when I was quite ignorant of all things, and I do not think I often smiled before you, Teacher, came to me."

"City Of Kind Hearts"

"He is very happy indeed at the kindergarten," she wrote the Editor of the *Boston Herald*, "and he is learning something every day. He has found out that doors have locks, and that little sticks can be got into the key-hole quite easily; but he does not seem very eager to get them out after they are in. He loves to climb the bed-posts, and unscrew the steam valves much better than to spell!

"He will learn fast enough by and by," was her confident conclusion.

She was right. Love, patience and skill eventually demolished the barriers that stood between Tommy Stringer and the world. Helen became proud of the boy she had rescued, and thanks to her eager campaign, the waif who had faced a desolate, unknowing lifetime spent in a dreary almshouse, now possessed a fund of his own of thirteen hundred dollars.

"It is beautiful to me to think that the death of my dear, brave, loving Lioness should be the means of bringing so much happiness into the life of little Tommy," Helen wrote to the Editor of *Forest and Stream*, when she sent him her receipt for his check.

Later she was fired with the inspiration to "help Mr. Anagnos raise money for the kindergarten." When she talked the matter over with her young friends, Caroline Derby and Mrs. Howe's granddaughter, Rosy Richards, they determined to hold a combination "Tea and Fair." Mrs. Mahlon D. Spaulding opened her home to them, and thanks to the many spirited letters Helen wrote, all of the famous, fashionable and wealthy Bostonians came—Bishop Phillips Brooks, Dr. Oliver Wendell Holmes, and Helen's cousin, Dr. Edward Everett Hale, heading the guest list—and when the affair was over, a joyous trio of girls could present Mr. Anagnos with the really remarkable sum of two thousand dollars.

"Boston is truly the City of Kind Hearts!" was Helen's joyous verdict.

CHAPTER · 13

"The
Frost
King"

WITH TOMMY STRINGER ESTABLISHED at the kindergarten, well on the way to becoming a friendly,
happy child; with Mr. Anagnos praising her for the
progress she had made that year, and everyone re-
marking on the improvement she had made in her
speech, Helen went home at the end of June a well
and happy girl. Even Annie felt more relaxed and
confident.

Once in Tuscumbia, however, she realized something was wrong. Kate Keller was sad, and the Captain nervous and troubled. A few days later, Mr. Keller shut all the children out and made an unhappy
confession to Annie. The Keller finances were in a

state of collapse. There could be no more trips to Boston even as "guests" of the school. It was a blow, and Annie would not deny it. Helen had been forging ahead so rapidly, and a blind pupil had to have expensive Braille and embossed books, besides other special equipment, but—she shrugged—it could be done.

But before she could offer any comfort, Kate Keller was choking, "There's more, Miss Annie!" She twisted her handkerchief in her nervous hands and the tears slipped uncontrollably down her face. "Miss Annie—there—isn't—even money to pay—your salary!"

And as Annie stared at her, Helen's mother put her head down and wept.

Perhaps Annie winced for a moment. And then she flung up her head. All her life it was Annie's philosophy that if disaster, despair or defeat struck, the only thing to do was to face it squarely and plunge on. Never a practical or a prudent person, several times in her life she negotiated "impossible" situations by this dauntless plunging-on process. Now she bent over Mrs. Keller. What she told her we do not know. We only know that she remained with the Kellers, and continued her forward march with Helen, and even helped Mrs. Keller preserve fruit and care for baby Phillips.

The family went to Fern Quarry again, and lingered until the mountains flamed with the glory of their autumn foliage. Annie was awed by their beauty, and day after day gave Helen vivid descriptions. Helen had always had an intense interest in color, and Annie's own blindness had taught her the desperate, unsatisfied longings the blind have to know what their friends are seeing.

As a result, wherever they went Helen clamored to know what was to be seen. What was the color of the horses? What color clothes were her friends wearing? How many babies were on the train? But nothing had ever impressed her so much as Annie's description of the Fern Quarry foliage. She seemed to be thrilled by it, and home again in Tuscumbia, she announced she was going to write a story.

She sat down with her Braille slate, and wrote as rapidly as her stiletto would prick out the letters. She was breathlessly absorbed, and the happy words flowed out of her fingers. They came easily, quickly, as she told all about the mighty King Frost who lived in his magnificent ice palace, guarded by "twelve soldierly-looking white bears," and how he came to cover the summer leaves with precious stones, rubies, emeralds, and gold.

She tingled with the exultation all writers instinctively have when they know they have written something good, and settled herself with eagerness to read it aloud to Annie, and when Annie checked her to correct her pronunciation, she was impatient. Annie was amazed at the real beauty and smoothness of the little story. Helen had written several stories before, and one, "Sister Mabel," had been published in *St. Nicholas*. And she had written many little essays, all of which were really astonishingly good. But this "Autumn Leaves" was the best of them all. How could a deaf-blind child of eleven create such a wonderful picture?

Helen took it proudly to the dinner table and read it aloud to the family. Her editor-father was beside himself with joy. Her mother asked thoughtfully, "Did you read anything like it in any book?"

The question surprised Helen. She shook her head emphatically. "Oh, no! It is my story, and I have written it for Mr. Anagnos as a birthday gift!"

She painstakingly copied the story in her printscript, and insisted upon carrying it to the post office and mailing it herself, chattering and dancing along, feeling as she wrote later, as though she were walking on air.

Ten days later Annie created a flurry of fear by being bitten by a dog suspected to be mad. The Pasteur serum hadn't reached the South, nor even Boston, so when Mr. Anagnos heard about the wound he commanded Annie to hurry to the Pasteur Institute in New York City, and ordered the doctor to send all bills to him.

Meanwhile he had been told that Helen and Annie could not accept his invitation to spend a third year at Perkins, and he promptly sent another, more urgent invitation, insisting that they come.

Then he wrote a special note to Annie, begging her not to worry:

> Pray do not have the least anxiety about the future. Be Captain Keller's circumstances what they may, Helen and you will not be allowed to suffer.

Mr. Anagnos had been working on his Report for 1891 when Helen's story reached him. He was enthralled by it and promptly decided to publish it in the Report. This particular report could almost have been called the Helen Keller Report rather than the Perkins Report, for out of three hundred and five pages, one hundred and forty six were paeans upon paeans of praise of Helen. Mr. Anagnos had told Annie he thought that, after a lapse of three years, it was time to bring the record of Helen's progress officially up to date, and had asked her to write an account of Helen's life since 1888. If he had been content to let her report stand by itself, there would have been a straightforward, vivid, accurate story, but Mr. Anagnos never knew that simplicity is the best policy. He injected so many lyrical comments of his own that when Annie read the report she wondered if it really was Helen's story hidden in this labyrinth of exaggeration.

> Helen's imagination is luxuriant. It is irrepressible, unconfinable. It is like a vast mirror of the mind, on which the images of external forms are reflected in perfect form and with amazing velocity . . .

Helen's writings show the fecundity of her imaginative power. They sparkle with perfect crystallizations of fancy's blossoms, which are sometimes huddled in clusters upon the blazing page.

Helen's thoughts dwell in a world of beauty and majesty, and she shines like a new resplendent gem in the treasure house of humanity. She is pure and fresh as a violet. . . . She is thoroughly imbued with the spirit of uprightness, fights heroically the battles of justice and equality.

This was horrible! Annie writhed over every fresh sentence. Helen was an exceptionally bright, eager and lovable child, but she was none of these sickening things. She was very human. Wasn't the truth wonderful enough?

Mr. Anagnos' rhapsodies went on page after page until Annie dropped the book, torn between half-hysterical laughter at the utter silliness of Mr. Anagnos' report and anger and indignation that her beautiful Helen should be pictured as such an insufferable plaster saint.

"She knows absolutely nothing of the unkindness, hostility, narrow-mindedness, and wickedness of the world around her!" Mr. Anagnos exclaimed.

Which wasn't in the least true, but if it had been, the poor child learned them all very shortly after the Report was published.

She had loved her little story, "Autumn Leaves" which Mr. Anagnos published as "The Frost King." She knew it was good and was pleased when people praised it. And then the terrible blow fell. One January morning when Annie went in to comb Helen's long hair, she was obliged to break the dreadful news to the child.

"Helen, someone has written Mr. Anagnos that your story, 'The Frost King,' is not your story at all. That it was published long ago in a book, and called 'Frost Fairies.' Think very, very hard. I never read you a story like that. But did anyone else?"

"Oh, no, no!" Helen protested. "I am sure I never heard it. I am perfectly sure I wrote the story myself. Oh, how could there be such a mistake? And now people will think I am untrue and wicked."

Annie tried to comfort her, but Helen was too hurt and grieved; and when she met Mr. Anagnos she knew he was very upset.

The unhappy truth was that Helen's "Frost King" was almost sentence for sentence the same story as "Frost Fairies," a chapter in a book, *Birdie and His Friends,* by Margaret T. Canby, which had appeared seven years before Helen was born.

But the mystery was how or where Helen had learned it. Annie had never even heard of the book, nor had Mrs. Keller. All Helen's relatives and friends shook their heads. The book—or the single story—wasn't in embossed or Braille print. How could the thing have happened? But it had, and there was no denying it. And Helen's tear-choked insistence that she never remembered hearing the story didn't help. The child herself sensed there was an unfriendly atmosphere rising around her. "My heart is full of tears," she wrote in her diary, "For I love the beautiful truth with all my heart . . . Mr. Anagnos is much troubled, and it grieves me that I have caused him such unhappiness."

Eventually it was Mrs. Hopkins who solved part of the puzzle. Racking her brains, she finally remembered that her daughter Florence had owned a copy of *Birdie and His Friends.* Also she recalled that during the summer of 1888 Annie had been obliged to leave Brewster for a couple of days to have her eyes treated, and during that time she, Mrs. Hopkins, had amused the little Helen by reading her stray stories from her daughter's books. "Frost Fairies" must have been one of them. And shortly after that she had given away all her daughter's books.

That meant that Helen had heard the story when she was eight years old. She hadn't even been enough impressed with the story itself to repeat it to Annie on Annie's return. The little fairy tale had simply dropped into her subconscious memory and remained there until it was wakened by Annie's description of the autumn foliage at Fern Quarry.

Annie breathed a thankful sigh of relief. It was easy to understand what had happened, especially when one knew Helen's ability to remember in detail anything she had heard. Mr. Anagnos certainly would understand. Indeed, he had extolled her remarkable powers of memory in his latest report.

And then the storm really broke. Helen was to have been the goddess Ceres in a pageant given by the Girls' Department on Washington's Birthday. At the rehearsal the night before the celebration one of the teachers found the child and began firing questions at her as to how she had gotten her ideas for "The Frost King," and in all innocence the child answered readily, "Teacher had talked to me about Jack Frost and his wonderful works, and told me how he had painted the leaves ruby, emerald, crimson, gold and brown, and all at once the story began coming to me——"

She had said enough. The teacher flew to Mr. Anagnos with the report that Helen had "confessed" that she did remember Annie had told her the "Frost Fairies" story.

Annie was appalled and incredulous when she heard that Mr. Anagnos had called an "investigating committee" of eight teachers, four blind and four sighted, to try the eleven-year-old child on the charge of "plagiarism."

A very frightened Helen was summoned, and Annie was ordered out of the room, and then the committee accused the child of having sent Mr. Anagnos a published story represented as her own in a deliberate attempt to deceive him, and then trying to lie her way out of it. In Mr. Anagnos' own report of the affair it was "a most rigid examination of about two hours' duration, during which all sorts of questions were asked with perfect freedom, but failed to elicit the least testimony convicting her teacher or anyone else of the intention to commit deceit."

For two hours the committee hammered at her until Helen felt the blood pounding in her ears. Her heart seemed to be tearing her body apart. Terrified and desperate—and alone—she felt the hostility all around her, and had the feeling that Mr. Anagnos was gazing at her reproachfully. At last she didn't even know what she said.

But they couldn't shake her story, and finally they let her go, a shaking, sobbing, dazed little girl who was beyond comprehending the words someone was spelling over and over into her hand: "You are a brave, brave little girl, and we are all so proud of you." She was even beyond responding to Annie's caresses, and lay on her bed in a semi-stupor. But that night fresh realization of the whole ugly business returned to stab at her, and she wept with such agony-wracked sobs that Annie, holding her, and Mrs. Hopkins, bending over her, were frightened. They had never known such heartbreak in a child.

She was too choked to speak, but over and over her fingers formed the words, "I never knew I had heard the story. I love the truth! I love the beautiful truth!"

She was so cold she thought she would die.

For all her steadfastness four of the committee voted that Helen had been deliberately deceitful;

four believed her innocent. Mr. Anagnos cast his vote in favor of Helen.

What was the root of it all? Had the storm been brewing for some time? Had it begun two years before with Annie's unfortunate remark that she had sole and complete charge over Helen? It must be admitted that their peculiar position at the school could have been a basis for biased feelings. Here was a former charity pupil of Perkins now a special teacher in charge of a brilliant child—and both of them had been at Perkins for over two years as guests. It cannot be denied that Helen rated high in her classes and attracted more attention than all the other pupils put together. And finally, there was Mr. Anagnos' extravagant account of her in his report. Had he sung her praises too much?

Despite Mr. Anagnos' writing that he was entirely convinced that Helen was unaware of ever having heard Miss Canby's story, and that he was satisfied that she "did love the beautiful truth," there was a complete change in the atmosphere at Perkins, and Helen was acutely conscious of it. Even when she went into Mr. Anagnos' office there was something menacing in the air. She could feel the wall of distrust and misgiving rising between them. Mr. Anagnos was still there, but her old friend was gone.

Two things about the "Frost King" episode have grieved Helen Keller all her life. The first is that some people openly cast doubts upon Annie's honesty; the other is the loss of Michael Anagnos' friendship. "He locked us out of his heart!" she has said.

And so at Perkins, which had been her "Place of Wonder, A real Enchanted Ground," she learned the lesson of "the unkindness, hostility, and narrow-mindedness of the world around her."

One of the strangest things of the whole strange affair was the attitude of Captain Keller: He wrote two letters to Mr. Anagnos, protesting Helen's innocence, but offering profuse apologies for the sorrow Helen had brought him.

But loyal and sympathetic friends gathered around Helen and Annie. Dr. Bell, in Boston at that time for litigation over some of his telephone patents, took time out from his business troubles to come and try to comfort them.

"We all do what Helen did." he exclaimed. "Our most original compositions are expressions derived from others."

But the most understanding words came from Margaret Canby:

If she had remembered and written down accurately a short story, and that soon after hearing it, it would have been a marvel; but to have heard the story once, three years ago, and in such a way . . . and then to reproduce it so vividly, even adding some touches of her own in perfect keeping with the rest, which really improve the original, is something very few girls of riper years and with every advantage of sight and hearing

could have done. Under these circumstances I do not
see how anyone can be so unkind as to call it plagiarism.
She stands *alone!* . . . Please give her my warm love,
and tell her not to feel troubled about it any more. No-
one shall be allowed to think it was wrong; and some
day she will write a great, beautiful story.

But perhaps Mark Twain, years later when he
read Helen's own account of the bitter affair,
summed up the "Plagiarism Court" episode best
when he wrote Helen, and called it "a collection of
decayed human turnips."

CHAPTER · 14

"Let Me
Not Break
Nor Bend—"

Listlessness fell over Helen and clung to her most of the summer. She had a terror of writing, even letters to her family and closest friends. "Suppose it should be found out that everything I say was written by someone long ago?" she asked Annie in despair.

And even when she was talking and a sudden idea flashed into her mind, she would falter, and then spell unobtrusively, "I'm not sure if this idea is my own!" It was a torment to think that she might be a thief, stealing someone else's thoughts.

And Annie was doing battle with her own fears. She was afraid of Helen's depression, and afraid that the same thing would happen again—and there would be no way to guard against it, for with Helen's expanding abilities she couldn't keep a check on everything her pupil read or heard. But she fought back her own distress and strove to draw the girl away from the shadow of her experience.

"You must remember what both Dr. Bell and Miss Canby said, Helen. And I know you have a fine mind with a' great many original thoughts in it. You may say the same things other people do—we all do that—but you can say them in a new way."

In her distraught frame of mind Helen could not study. She had disgraced herself. She had brought suspicion and sorrow upon her dearest friends. "No child ever drank deeper of the cup of bitterness than I did," she confessed later. Once she told Phillips Brooks, "I am always happy." She would never be able to say that again. Now she needed all the love, understanding, and gentle help her friends could give her.

As for Annie, she eased the tension in her soul "in wild and dangerous horseback rides through the woods."

In the midst of this difficult time *The Youth's Companion* asked Helen to write a sketch of her life. She shrank from the idea involuntarily, but Annie and her mother coaxed her into thinking about it. It would be, they knew, the best thing she could do —perhaps the only thing to free her of her torturing doubts and fears. Finally, to please them, just a year after she had so gaily written "The Frost King," with the autumn leaves rustling under feet and the musk-scented grapes ripening on the arbor, Helen sat down to write her little autobiography.

She did not write gaily and swiftly now, but timidly, fearfully. Never again would she write with that joyous abandon that had gone into "The Frost King." Sometimes in the midst of a paragraph an imp of fear would clutch her hand, and she would put her head down, exclaiming, "I cannot. Please do not make me!"

But Annie resolutely urged her to go on. If Helen could complete this sketch, Annie thought, she would regain her mental footing. And again she was right. The little sketch received a warm welcome from *The Youth's Companion,* and didn't betray any of the hesitancy Helen had felt when she worked on it. The writing really had done Helen good. She was ready to pick up her lessons now, although personally Annie was not at all satisfied with the outlook of Helen's education. There seemed no definite goal now to aim at.

The next year, however, when Helen was thirteen, was a happier one, thanks to Dr. Bell. First he invited Helen and Annie to be his guests in Washington and attend President Cleveland's second inauguration. Then he and Helen planned a surprise for Annie, and took her to see Niagara Falls. Helen was thrilled when she stood on the point that overhangs the American Falls and felt the air vibrate and the earth tremble. Crossing over to the Canadian side, she cried, "God Save the Queen!"

"Why, you little traitor." said Annie.

Their hotel was so near the river that Helen could feel it rush past by placing her hand on the window. She told her mother later, "I could hardly realize that it was water that I felt rushing and plunging with impetuous fury at my feet. It seemed as if it were some living thing rushing on to some terrible fate."

Some of the people they met asked Helen somewhat stupid questions. One woman was surprised to find that she loved flowers "when you cannot see their beautiful colors—but no doubt you feel their colors with your fingers." Then there was the gentleman who asked what beauty could mean to her. Helen was baffled, but after a minute she told him she imagined it was a form of goodness—and then, Helen told her mother, he "went away!"

In August Dr. Bell took them to the World's Columbian Exposition in Chicago. The president of the fair gave her a note to all the exhibitors that she was to be allowed to handle everything wherever it was possible. Watching her, people exclaimed to Annie, "She sees more with her fingers than we do with our eyes!"

Everything fascinated her. She loved the Indian bazaar, "with its Shivas and elephant-gods," and the model of Cairo made Egypt come alive to her; she went aboard a Viking ship, and sailed in the Venice lagoon each evening. In the electrical building she examined the telephones, autophons and phonographs, and Dr. Bell made her understand how messages were sent on wires to "mock space and outrun time." She especially loved the French bronzes. At the Cape of Good Hope exhibit, she was enthralled with the mining of diamonds. She touched the moving machinery to see how diamonds were weighed, cut and polished. She searched in the washings for a diamond, and found one—the only true diamond, they told her, that had ever been found in the United States.

The trip had been unadulterated joy for Helen, but it brought home to Annie how much there was for Helen to discover and learn in the world and how very incompetent Annie was to help her do it. She must have confessed this to Dr. Bell, and asked his help. She "bewailed her mockery of an education," and he assured her:

You were at least not hampered by preconceived notions, and I think that an advantage. You did not take to your task standardized ideas, and your own individuality was so ingrained that you didn't try to repress Helen's. You must not lay too much stress on what you were not taught by others. What we learn from others is of less value than what we teach ourselves!

But he did understand and agree with what

Annie felt about Helen's education, and appreciated the advantages to her exceptionally eager mind of associating with the literary people gathered in Boston. She really was ready now for something more than Annie could give. Yes, Dr. Bell knew Captain Keller couldn't afford to do anything more for Helen, but something must be arranged. Helen Keller must have the best.

Whether Dr. Bell was responsible for what happened next is not clear; but Helen and Annie received an invitation from Mr. William Wade, the giver of Lioness and Neddy, to spend several months with the Wade family in Hulton, Pennsylvania. Helen was delighted. They had visited the Wade house twice on the way home from Perkins, and it was a wonderful place, with lively children, many dogs and thirteen donkeys! For some reason Mr. Wade was especially interested in blind children, and Helen's case appealed to him particularly. He went into action at once.

"We have a neighbor, a Dr. John Irons, a Presbyterian minister," he told Annie, "who would make an excellent tutor for Helen if he can be persuaded to teach her."

Dr. Irons was called for a consultation, and he and Helen were friends almost at once. He accepted the task promptly, and Helen was thrilled. Her visit to the World's Fair had stirred all her old interest to know "many things."

187

"Dear Diary," Helen wrote, "today is the thirteenth of October, 1893, and I have pleasant news for you. My studies began today, and I am very, very glad. I study Arithmetic, Latin, History, Geography and Literature. I am glad because I want to know more and more about this beautiful, wonderful world. . . . I used to say I did not like Arithmetic, but now I see what a good, useful study it is. I try to be very calm and patient when the examples seem very hard, but in spite of my efforts to keep my mind in the right place, it will flutter like a little bird in a cage and try to escape."

Despite all her efforts, she never learned to really like mathematics of any kind. She wasn't interested in Latin grammar, either. Picking up French had been such a game with her that it seemed silly wasting time dissecting every word she came across.

"I might just as well take my pet cat apart!" she said wryly. "Order, vertebrate; division, quadruped; class, mammalia; genus, felinus; species, cat; individual, Tabby. Why not just read Latin?"

But Latin really became her favorite subject. She loved the time spent with Dr. Irons, and he was enthusiastic about her. When Mr. Wade complimented him on his work with Helen, he answered, "It would be a sad botcher who couldn't make a success out of such material."

Of the three, Annie's work was much the hardest. Naturally Dr. Irons didn't know the finger alphabet, and Helen's lip-reading accomplishment was too slow and laborious a process, especially with a stranger, so Annie sat beside her at each session, spelling out all Dr. Irons said. She had to listen and interpret to Helen, and in many cases translate Helen's speech for Dr. Irons, and then read Helen's assignments to her. It was far from being the easiest work in the world, especially for one whose eyes blurred and burned, but Helen was leaping forward. Annie counted that pure gain.

And then, for some unknown reason, the Kellers summoned them back to Tuscumbia in February. Annie went in a very dark frame of mind.

If the truth be told, it would appear that Annie never liked the South. She once complained to Helen that "life in Tuscumbia was as monotonous as the song of the whippoorwill."

Now after a three-months' glimpse of the kind of education Helen could have, and the work she could accomplish, Annie felt "like a ship without a rudder."

Back in Alabama she and Helen carried on as best they could. Now Annie was devoting much time to Helen's voice and lip reading, desperately wishing that she had some expert help. Once she exclaimed in despair, "I would give up all happiness in this world and the next if it would give you natural speech!"

"Oh, Teacher, no, you must not," cried the frightened Helen.

Another day when Helen had practiced her voice lesson to the point where tiredness suddenly stiffened the muscles of her face, tongue and throat simultaneously, Annie's nerves betrayed her to tears. "Oh, Helen, stop it! Stop!" she begged. "You look petrified!"

She must have help—she must—if Helen was to become an independent and useful person in the world, and not always be dependent on the charity of others. She must have a great deal more education to fit her to be a useful citizen.

Little by little she took up the hard duty of explaining this to Helen—how completely dependent she would always be physically, and so she must prepare to be independent mentally and financially. How would she handle this part of her life?

"I can read." Helen announced confidently. "I can read, and I will devour every book I can find!"

"That is a good way to get educated," replied Annie, "but it is not enough. If you grow up to be a bookworm, what use will you be to the world? You must think of something more."

Annie also had to think of something more. The concern kept her awake. Helen needed help. Perhaps most of all she had to have help with her speech and her lip reading for, after all, comparatively few people knew the finger alphabet. But where were they to find this help? And how?

It was Dr. Bell who came to the rescue once

more. In July, 1894, Annie was invited to speak before the American Association to Promote the Teaching of Speech to the Deaf, at their meeting in Chautauqua, New York. Of course Helen accompanied her. At the last minute Annie was so overcome with shyness and nervousness that Dr. Bell read her speech on educating Helen. In it Annie made a rather surprising statement: she said she thought entirely too much had been published about Helen Keller, and she would be happy if she could convince her audience that Helen was not an "extraordinary genius," but simply a very bright and lovely child, and that her so-called marvelous accomplishments consisted only in her being able to speak and write the language of her country with greater ease and fluency than the average child of her age.

Annie was certainly wrong. Besides her gift for English, Helen possessed a natural flair for any language, a remarkable memory and strong determination. But perhaps her greatest asset has always been her winning and compelling personality.

Dr. Bell had always had an outspoken admiration for Annie's methods in teaching Helen, and he believed her ideas should be in the hands of everyone teaching the deaf, but perhaps he had a double purpose in bringing her and Helen to this meeting. It was there that they met John Wright and Dr. Thomas Humanson, who were planning to open a new oral school for the deaf in New York City. The two men heard Helen speak and watched her lip-read, and told Annie, "We believe that with our new methods Helen's voice may become a natural one."

CHAPTER · 15

Wagon To The Star

October, 1894:—Helen and Annie were established in the Wright-Humanson Oral School for the Deaf in New York City. The kindly godfathers who maneuvered this venture shunned publicity, but Helen's steadfast friend, "King John" Spaulding of Boston, certainly was one, and she strongly suspected that Dr. Bell had had a hand in it. But at any rate they were there.

"The school is very pleasant," Helen wrote to a friend, "and, bless you, quite fashionable. . . . I enjoy my singing lessons with Dr. Humanson more than I can say."

Dr. Humanson was trying "vocalizing exercises"

to teach her to control her voice and help her have a higher and clearer pitch. The lip-reading process bothered her most of all. She had always been able to catch separate words, but connected speech was a real ordeal. It required all Dr. Humanson's patient help and Annie's encouragement, added to Helen's own high courage, to press on amid failure and utter weariness. This was the most tiring, nerve-wracking task Helen had ever undertaken. It was slow and difficult, and sometimes it seemed of no use. There were many times when Helen was perilously close to tears.

Difficulties, however, were no fearsome strangers to either Helen or Teacher. Long ago they had discovered that the thing to do is to recognize and accept them—and then move either over or around them. Helen might be disappointed at the slowness of her progress, but she was undaunted. And at the end of six months, Dr. Humanson was able to report she understood the speech of her teachers and the other pupils accurately, although the lip-reading process was still slow and laborious work.

Also her speech was improved. It was clearer—the pitch higher, and the tone more flexible. She could even, when she touched the throat of a singer, detect changes in pitch as slight as a halftone, and imitate the same pitch herself.

It was a good school and must have been a pleasant one. The pupils were taken on excursions to the Statue of Liberty, dog shows in Madison Square

Garden, and the theater. Helen was a pupil there two years—with Annie sitting beside her in her classes—and she stood high among the deaf pupils, just as she had among the blind at Perkins.

Socially, New York was just as friendly as Boston. In some way Helen and Annie became friends with Lawrence Hutton, the literary critic, and his lovely wife, Eleanor, and were entertained at their house often. It was at the Huttons' that they met Mark Twain, Henry Van Dyke, Woodrow Wilson, Kate Douglas Wiggin Riggs, Joseph Jefferson, Ellen Terry, and Sir Henry Irving.

At one of the first Hutton parties, someone wanted to see if Helen could recognize the people she had met for the first time that afternoon by the clasp of their hands. When Mark Twain reached her he decided to be different, and instead of taking her inquiring hand, he patted her lightly on the head.

"Oh!" she exclaimed instantly, "That is Mr. Clemens!"

She described the afternoon in an excited letter to her mother:

New York, March 31, 1895
Teacher and I spent the afternoon at Mr. Hutton's, and had a most delightful time. . . . We met Mr. Clemens and Mr. Howells there. I never thought that I should see them and talk to them; and I can scarcely realize that this great pleasure has been mine. . . . I wonder that I, only a little girl of fourteen, should come

195

into contact with so many distinguished people. I do
realize I am a very happy child. The two distinguished
authors were very gentle and kind. . . . Mr. Clemens
told us many entertaining stories and made us laugh
until we cried. I wish you could have seen and heard
him. I think he is very handsome indeed. Teacher said
she thought he looked a little like Paraderski (if that's
the way to spell the name.) Mr. Hutton gave me a
lovely little glass, shaped like a thistle, which had belonged to his dear mother, as a souvenir of my delightful visit.

A spark of instantaneous friendship had leaped
between Mark Twain and Helen and Annie which
glowed for the rest of his life. Cynical and sarcastic
though he could be, Samuel Clemens always possessed a heart that was quickly and easily touched
by anything moving, and he found something in
both Helen and Annie that he recognized as genuine
and lovely. Many people had eyes only for Helen.
Samuel Clemens was one of the few who saw Annie
as an outstanding and lovable person in her own
right. Helen he loved. Annie he appreciated as few
others ever did.

Another person to appreciate her was Ellen Terry.
When they met she kissed Annie and said softly,
"I don't know whether I am glad to see you or not
—I am so ashamed of myself when I think of what
you have done."

They had two very happy years at the Wright-
Humanson School. And then Helen had an amaz-

ing, breath-taking ambition. She wanted to go to college! Years before, as a little girl, she had confidently announced, "Some day I am going to go to college. I am going to go to Harvard."

She could laugh about that now. Harvard wasn't likely to open its doors, but what about Harvard's sister college, Radcliffe?

At first it seemed impossible to everyone, including lionhearted Annie. Helen had never had precollege courses. She had never been in classes for normal girls. She would need much more preparation. Could she—could Annie— keep up the pace? And of course—perhaps the biggest stumbling block of all—there was no money. And her dear, generous Boston friend, John Spaulding, was dead.

But one thing Helen Keller has always possessed: influential friends who could step forward in her hour of need. First it was Alexander Graham Bell, who said she could be educated; then Michael Anagnos, and John Spaulding. Now it was Mrs. Hutton who stepped into the breach and undertook to raise a fund that would carry Helen through college and keep her and her "essential companion, Miss Sullivan," on financially safe ground.

There probably had been people, even distinguished folk, who had gone to the parties or the teas where they knew Helen was to be because they were fascinated by her story and were eager to see the Wonder Child, but most of them, once they had been with her, forgot that she was a prodigy and surrendered to her simply because she was a joyous, natural, eager-minded girl who seemed to be brimming with interest in everybody else. When the time came there were several outstanding persons on Eleanor Hutton's committee. Dr. Bell, of course, William Dean Howells, Bishop Greer, and others who thought that educating Helen would be a good investment for America.

Annie's own heart faltered at the thought of another school. She always hated fixed routines and a set course of study, and there was no ignoring the fact that her eyes were growing worse.

"Sometimes," she told Mr. Hitz, the superintendent of the Volta Bureau for the Deaf in Washington, "it seems to me I cannot endure the thought of going to another school, and at such times it seems as if I had better let another person take my place."

There didn't seem to be another person, and she began investigating various schools. The Cambridge School for Young Ladies was recommended to her by Elizabeth Cary Agassiz, who had been president of Radcliffe, and she went to see Arthur Gilman, the principal, who was frankly very skeptical. Oh, yes, he understood that Helen was an extraordinary girl —but college for a deaf-blind pupil? It simply wasn't practical. However, he would meet and talk to Helen if Miss Sullivan wished—and when he did he called her "this marvelous girl" and welcomed her into the Cambridge School in September 1896.

And now, for the first time in their lives, Helen

and Annie were living and working with normal girls of Helen's own age. Helen was elated, for it seemed to mean that she was becoming "like other people!" But elation never lingers, and two months later Helen was confessing the obstacles that were rearing their heads:

It takes me a long time to prepare my lessons, because I have to have every word of them spelled into my hand. Not one of the text-books which I use is in raised print; so of course my work is harder than it would be if I could read my lessons by myself. But it is harder for Teacher than it is for me, because the strain on her poor eyes is so great, and I cannot help worrying about them. Sometimes it really seems as if the tasks we have set ourselves are more than we can accomplish.

More than once Annie went to bed wondering if she would wake blind the next morning. But they went on, and gradually things eased a little. Braille books came from Philadelphia and England, thanks to Mr. Wade; kindly Frau Grote, the German teacher, learned the finger alphabet so that she could give Helen special lessons in German; some of the girls learned it as well, and the rest of the teachers and pupils soon learned to understand Helen's imperfect speech. As for Mr. Gilman, by this time he had become so enthusiastic that he had learned the finger alphabet himself in order to talk to Helen and teach her the English courses.

At Christmas time Mrs. Keller and Mildred came up to spend the holidays in Cambridge with Helen and Annie. Captain Keller had died in September. Mr. Gilman must have been impressed with ten-year-old Mildred, for he asked Mrs. Keller to let her join Helen in the school. He must have been repaid by the flashing joy in Helen's face, for Helen had a passionate love for this little sister, and had always been lonely for her during their enforced separations. As for Annie, she frankly adored the child.

The next months were happy ones. Helen's studies seemed to be easier. She had her precious little sister with her, and she was learning that she could even join normal girls when they went coasting or hiking—yes, even riding a tandem bicycle.

But perhaps the happiest day at Cambridge was the afternoon Tommy Stringer was brought to see her. She knew of his progress through Mrs. Hopkins and her other old friends at Perkins, and finally wrote Tommy and his teachers an invitation to come to Cambridge.

Flushed and breathless, she kissed the teachers, but her hands roved eagerly until they touched the close-cropped head of the small boy. Joy flashed into her face, and someone remarked that it remained shining throughout the visit.

"What a fine big boy he is. The dear little fellow." She cried excitedly when she could find breath enough to use her voice. The questing hands touched his face and shoulders and reached for one chubby hand and began to spell her excited greeting. Tom answered, but he wanted to do some investigating of his own, and he was spelling with one hand while "looking" at Helen with the other.

When he reached her hair, his fingers lingered. "Soft," he commented. "Nice. Pretty."

So intent was Helen on their rapid exchange of words and examinations that Annie's interrupting touch had to be repeated twice before the girl was aware of it. "You and Tommy will be able to talk quite as well if you sit down, Helen."

Annie joined in the teachers' laughter, but she watched with quick tears as Helen repeated her remark and then piloted Tommy to the wide window seat where they could "talk" without interruption. She, too, was remembering the fragile, helpless mite Tommy had been six years before. Was it really possible that that Tommy Stringer was the intelligent, sturdy Tommy Stringer who was talking into Helen's hand with such rapid assurance?

Tommy was telling her of his pet play. Like many children who are lonely or restricted, he had built up a world of his own. "New Garden," he called it.

"What a romantic name!" Helen declared. "Tell me all about it."

Somehow the child sensed that here was a person who would understand and not laugh at him. Wiggling with satisfaction, he poured the whole story into her hands. New Garden was a mansion containing ninety-four rooms, which he had filled with imaginary people.

Miss Bull told Helen of Tommy's odd habit of nicknaming his teachers and friends after animals or insects. One teacher he called "Fly," another "Cow," another "Horse." Helen was amused, and promptly asked him if he had a nickname for her? The child nodded emphatically and spelled "Blackbird." No one knew why until Helen touched the bird-shaped pin at her throat.

At the end of the visit she gave him a miniature carved Swiss chalet, and was delighted when he informed her it was a house with a barn, and little, little stairs and a fence.

Following his rapid words, Helen must have been proud and thrilled at the results of her "Tommy Fund."

June came, and examinations. The Harvard-Radcliffe entrance examinations were divided into two parts, "preliminaries" and "finals." Now was the time to take the preliminaries. And here Annie couldn't help. The college authorities said it must be someone else. So it was Mr. Gilman, with his slower spelling, who would read the examination papers to her.

Because she would have to use a typewriter Helen was given a small room to herself on the morning of June 29, 1897 (just two days after her seven-

teenth birthday). Seated at her typewriter, with
Mr. Gilman beside her, she waited. At nine o'clock
the sealed examinations left Harvard and were
brought to the Cambridge school. Mr. Gilman had
posted a man outside the door with strict orders
to admit no one except college officers. Taking the
papers, Mr. Gilman sat down and began spelling
the Advanced German examination into Helen's
hand—her lip reading was too slow and uncertain
to be trusted. He read the whole paper through
first, and then repeated sentence by sentence, and
Helen repeated the words aloud to make sure she
had understood.

She was tense, and little drops of perspiration
gathered on her forehead; her left hand opened
and closed as though she was trying to clutch at
ideas. This was it. This was the test that would
determine whether Annie Sullivan had been right
in her methods, and whether a deaf-blind girl had
a right to try to enter college at all.

German had become her favorite and easiest subject, but this was a stiff examination, and Helen
knew it. She said one swift prayer: "Help me—help
me do my best." And then she began to write. Her
breath came unevenly, but the fingers on the typewriter keys didn't falter. Mr. Gilman spelled as
steadily as he could, and Helen wrote. Finally the
two-and-a-half-hour ordeal was over.

They had a day's respite, and then came the
Latin examination. It wasn't easy, but it wasn't like

the German, and there was good news that morning. One of the professors came to tell Mr. Gilman she had passed in German. The other examinations she took easily, even though there were questions on some subjects in English history with which she was unfamiliar. But when her nine hours were over Helen had passed in every subject and had taken "honors" in English and German.

Helen had proved she could compete with seeing, hearing girls. She'd proved her right to enter college. She had justified Annie's unorthodox methods of teaching.

CHAPTER · 16

The Eighth Of December

HELEN RETURNED TO THE SCHOOL confident and happy. The examinations were behind her and she had done well. Mildred was with her, and Teacher's eyes were better after their summer rest.

But with the beginning of this new year, Helen wasn't doing very well in school. The printing of some Braille books in London was delayed and she was obliged to have a special Greek cylinder made for her typewriter. She also had to learn to use a new machine for embossing algebra, and to follow Annie's ingenious method of constructing geometric figures with wires on a cushion. Later Miss Hall, the physics teacher, learned Braille and prepared the figures and patterns in physics and astronomy.

So perhaps it wasn't surprising that Helen's averages weren't as impressive as they had been the first year. Nevertheless, Annie was stunned when Mr. Gilman informed her he had come to the conviction that Helen was being worked altogether too hard, and that he intended keeping her in the Cambridge School another three years.

Annie protested, but Mr. Gilman turned very cool, and made a gesture of dismissal. The matter was closed, for everyone.

Upset and unhappy, Annie had no desire to spend the rest of her life in schools. She returned to their room to help Helen with her history assignment. A few days later a slight illness overtook Helen and, never very fond of mathematics at any time, she had a bad hour with her geometry. The day happened to be a Friday, so Annie put her to bed for the weekend. When Mr. Gilman heard of it, he summoned Annie and addressed her curtly:

"Miss Sullivan, I am more than ever sure that Helen is working too hard, and I cannot be a party to it. Geometry and astronomy were too much for her to handle. They are being taken out of her program." Then, as Annie opened her lips, the principal shut his. "There is nothing more to be said, Miss Sullivan."

There was a strangeness in the atmosphere about them now. Both Annie and Helen felt it and were taut and miserable. And then a fortnight later, on December 8, 1897, a date neither of them ever forgot, and both shuddered to remember, Annie had another summons from Mr. Gilman. When she appeared, he greeted her coldly.

"Sit down, Miss Sullivan. I have something most unpleasant to say to you. However, it must be said. I have written to Mrs. Keller, and mind you, I did it only after much deliberation, but I found it was my duty to inform her that you are treating Helen cruelly, making her life a perfect grind, and that her child's health is in a very precarious condition."

All Annie's vehement, aggressive Irish spirit flared.

"Mr. Gilman—Mr. Gilman, how dared you lie so? I shall take Helen and Mildred out of your school and home to their mother this very day and tell her the truth—" She leaped to her feet, but he waved his hand and lifted a yellow paper from his desk.

"I think you will not, Miss Sullivan. No, I am quite sure you will not. And if you will read this, you will understand why I am so certain."

Trembling now, Annie had to wait until her eyes, always blurred by emotion, cleared to some extent, and then the bitter, incredible words jumped and danced before her. For the telegram was signed by Kate Keller, and gave Arthur Gilman authority to take complete charge of her daughter Helen.

"And now, Miss Sullivan, I am informing you that

you will leave this school at once." Mr. Gilman's voice could be very suave. "You may send for your possessions at your convenience, but you are to go immediately."

Somehow a broken, stumbling Annie obeyed him. Dazed, drained of all sensations and all thought, numb and physically ill, she stumbled down the streets. What had happened? Why had it happened? She came to the shore of the Charles River, and her feet involuntarily moved to the brink. Annie Sullivan never was a particularly religious woman, but she said afterward that it was as if an angel suddenly stood between her and the river, and a hand thrust her back, and very distinctly she heard a voice saying, "No, not yet. Go *on!*"

She went on. Almost by blind instinct she found the home of their friends, Mr. and Mrs. Richard Derby Fuller. They helped her send telegrams to Mrs. Keller, Dr. Bell, Mrs. Hutton, and Mr. Joseph Chamberlin, the "Listener" of the *Boston Transcript*. And the next morning she gathered her courage in both hands and returned to the Cambridge School, demanding to see the two Kellers.

"I will not leave until I do see them. You will have to carry me out by force." And under the fire in her eyes and the sound of steel in her voice, the maid who had been barring her way quailed and took her to the two girls.

Meanwhile Mr. Gilman had tried to persuade

Helen and Mildred to go home with him to his own house, but they were frightened, and refused.

"Not without Teacher." Helen insisted.

Annie found Mildred tearstained and shaking with sobs. Helen was white and tense, and had neither eaten nor slept. She had refused to budge. It was so that Mr. Chamberlin found them in the afternoon. Seeing how distraught they were, he persuaded Mr. Gilman to let him take charge of them and take them to his home, Red Farm, in Wrentham. It was there Mrs. Keller, who had taken the first train north, and Mr. Hitz, who came from Washington at Dr. Bell's request, found them.

Mrs. Keller was in tears. She was appalled at herself for having jumped to over-hasty conclusions on the strength of Mr. Gilman's letter, and after the impulse that prompted her to send the telegram had subsided she had been overcome by the "realization of the injustice and cruelty" of what she had done. She had been preparing to come to Cambridge when she received Annie's poignant telegram, "We need you."

"I do not need to be told that if you realized there was danger to Helen not for your right arm would you let her do it." Kate Keller declared to Annie. "I always think of Helen as partly your child. You know how largely I have left her to you, and what faith and confidence I have in you. Do not imagine I have any save feelings of love for you."

209

As for Helen, her mother thought she was "in perfect physical condition, and if she shows any evidence of nervous prostration or overwork, I cannot discover it."

Her interview with Mr. Gilman must have left that gentleman slightly dizzy. She told him in no uncertain terms that he had caused her much unnecessary distress and had cruelly misused the authority she had given him. That she had never dreamed of having Helen and Annie separated. And then she drew herself up with all the dignity of a Southern aristocrat.

"I thank you for all you did for my children during Helen's first year here. I will always appreciate it. But I want it understood that any attempt to separate Helen from Miss Sullivan meets with my unqualified condemnation. I am removing my children from your school. Good day, sir."

She took Mildred and departed for Tuscumbia. The Chamberlins had asked her to allow Helen and Annie to remain at Red Farm while their friends mapped out the best way for Helen to continue her college preparation.

It was one time in her life when Annie could have the good feeling that many people were her stanch friends and were standing solidly behind her. Mr. Hitz, Superintendent of the Volta Bureau in Washington, heartily approved of the way she had acted. So did Kate Keller and the Chamberlins.

The Eighth Of December

Mrs. Hutton wrote Mr. Gilman "it would be disastrous to Helen and unjustly cruel to Miss Sullivan to separate them," and besides, the contributions made to their fund had been made "with the express understanding it was for their joint support." She told Annie and Helen that she would engage a tutor to go on with Helen's courses. And Dr. Bell was vehement in his praise of Annie.

Helen and Annie had good times at Red Farm. The Chamberlins were a gay, warmly understanding family. Each one spoke so distinctly that Helen could read their lips easily, and they understood her. Betty, the oldest daughter, grew skillful in taking her about, describing the hills and King Philip's Pond. She helped Helen join in games and took her tobogganing. Each day Betty, Helen, and Annie would bundle up warmly and join a group of Betty's friends at the top of the steep hill near the Chamberlin house. While someone balanced the toboggan on the very crest, they would scramble to take their places. The glorious, breathless downward swoop as the toboggan swept over the smooth-packed run, leaping an upward mound, and then skimming far onto the frozen lake, exhilarated Helen. She never had enough of it. She even enjoyed toiling up the hill with the feel of the sharp, clean wind on her cheeks, and the tingling of her fingers. This was something she had missed in the schools—an active part in glorious outdoor doings. Afterward it was fun to snuggle down before a great fire and feel its warmth encircling her while she popped corn for the others.

Annie wasn't far behind in her enthusiasm. She instinctively felt at home with the Chamberlins and it was the first time in more than three years she and Helen had lived in a house! With the Chamberlins she could indulge in the luxury of being herself and unburdening her soul. She had always chafed under the necessary restrictions and routines of both the Wright-Humanson and the Gilman schools, and she had never felt at home with the teachers.

"Say what you will," she said with a grimace, "I never was cut out to be a schoolmarm."

Under the stimulating and understanding influence of the Chamberlin household Annie shed a little of the combative spirit she had needed for years, and by spring she had become joyously alive, and was surprising everybody with the sparkling charm of her personality. Helen remarked that it was wonderful how a little tact and understanding could "smooth out Teacher's soul-wrinkles."

Meanwhile, following Mrs. Hutton's instructions, Annie had found a highly recommended tutor in Boston, Merton S. Keith, who said he certainly would try to help Helen enter Radcliffe. He came for a three-hour period once a week while the girls stayed at Red Farm, and concentrated on Greek and mathematics. He found that Helen could race swiftly ahead in Greek. "If it is true," she commented, "that the violin is the most perfect of musical instruments, then Greek must be the violin of human thought." But in mathematics she was simply deplorable, and she confessed it.

"I cannot see why it is so very important to know that the lines drawn from the extremities of the base of an isosceles triangle to the middle points of the opposite sides are equal. The knowledge doesn't make life any sweeter or happier, does it?"

Eventually Mr. Keith managed to make algebra and geometry penetrate her brain, but they were never the delight languages were. "Horrid hobgoblins," she called them.

The three-hour periods were too long. Mr. Keith never learned the finger alphabet, and Annie once again acted as interpreter. She was almost exhausted at the end of the lessons. Added to the actual labor of spelling was the fact that Annie knew little about the mathematical problems, and cared less, and the Greek was just a maze of meaningless words to her. In addition she had to look up hundreds of words in the Greek lexicons!

Even Helen, eager as she was to press on to Radcliffe, was glad when June came and they could revel in outdoor life all day. She learned to swim and dive that summer, and to row her own boat around the lake. She loved canoeing—"particularly

213

on moonlight nights," she told one astonished friend. Another thing that startled everyone was her bicycle riding. Charles Dudley Warner asked her if she would like to own one, and she promptly told him yes. So he gave her a tandem, and she and Annie rode it. And like everyone else, she fell off sometimes.

After vacation they left Red Farm, rather reluctantly, for a small place in Boston where Mr. Keith would be more accessible. He came five days a week now, and added English history, literature, French and Latin to Helen's subjects. And then in June, 1899, it was time for the final entrance examinations.

But now Radcliffe hurled a bomb at them by insisting that a "perfect stranger read the examination papers to Miss Keller."

Someone suggested one of the teachers from Perkins, Mr. Eugene Vining, a teacher who never had happened to meet Helen, so Mr. Vining was engaged to go with Helen to Radcliffe on the Examination Days. He didn't know the finger alphabet, so he would copy the papers in Braille, and then Helen would write her answers on the typewriter. It was an awkward, cumbersome and irritating method, but in the face of Radcliffe's adamant stand there was no way around it.

Then, exactly two days before the first examination, a new complication stunned Helen. Mr. Vining knew only American Braille! Helen herself could read books in five raised types; New York Point, English and American Braille, Moon, and Boston Line embossed letters, but it happened that all her mathematical work had been done in English Braille —and the signs and symbols are completely different in the American system.

Desperate and alarmed, she sent Mr. Vining a hurried note for help, and he dispatched a chart of the American signs by return mail. Frantically Helen set to work learning them that night. She was worried and full of doubts by the time she reached the college the next morning. She had no difficulty in reading Mr. Vining's Braille for the language and history papers, but with mathematics she was up against not only her old bugaboo, but a strange system as well. It was tormenting and bewildering. She thought she had known the signs perfectly last night; now she tried feverishly to understand them, and their meaning escaped her. Her work was painfully slow. She read the examples again and again before they made sense. Her fingers felt cramped and stiff. She searched dizzily for answers that wouldn't come.

When it was over she let her hands fall limply into her lap and sat despondent. Just how miserably had she failed?

A few days later a trembling Annie opened the stiff envelope from Radcliffe College.

Valiant Companions

RADCLIFFE COLLEGE
CERTIFICATE OF ADMISSION
CAMBRIDGE JULY 4, 1899
HELEN ADAMS KELLER
IS ADMITTED TO THE FRESHMAN CLASS
IN RADCLIFFE COLLEGE.
AGNES IRWIN
DEAN OF RADCLIFFE COLLEGE

Miss Keller passed with credit in Advanced Latin.

CHAPTER · 17

The Story Of My Life

ANNIE'S FINGERS TREMBLED so that she could scarcely shape the words of victory. And then she thrust the precious sheet into Helen's hand and guided her forefinger across the glorious words.

A great flood of triumph surged over them both as they hugged each other. It was true. Together they had waged a battle against every obstacle in the book—rebuffs, almost insurmountable physical handicaps, drudgery that would have daunted a day laborer, weariness, tragedy. If Annie knew in her heart that she had done her eyes inestimable harm in helping Helen toward this victory, she brushed the thought aside. Nothing was worth considering today except the one glorious fact, that

Helen held in her hand the "Open Sesame" to college!

Today she didn't even flinch at the prospect of four more pent-up years. Today was a day of victory, and ahead lay a long, joyous summer at Lake Wollomonapoag, the lovely woodsy spot where Annie herself had rented a camp, and invited Kate Keller and her three children to be her guests.

Everyone was enthralled with Wollomonapoag. The lake was beautiful, cradled by mountains and surrounded by fragrant woods. Helen had her own boat, the *Naiad*, and delighted to row her sister and brother around the lake. With thirteen-year-old Mildred to steer, she could do it with perfect ease and safety. Annie also had a canoe and a raft, and swimming-wings for the benefit of her guests—and there were many of them! The Chamberlins came, and friends from Wrentham and Cambridge. They bathed, swam, played water polo, and had canoe races. And Annie, especially, was a born mermaid. One day she did frighten the Kellers out of their wits. She and Helen and Phillips were swimming one afternoon, and suddenly little Phillips grabbed his sister's hand and put it to his lips. She felt his face twisted with fear as he blurted, "Sis Helen! I—don't see Teacher!"

"We must get Mother!" Helen gasped. Hand in hand they ran wildly up the wharf shrieking their mother's name. Luckily she was within earshot and found help almost at once. Several men launched the *Naiad* and rowed swiftly around the lake. When they did find Annie she was at the point of exhaustion. But the next day she was swimming again, undaunted.

It was a happy summer. More than once Annie and Kate Keller, watching the tall, slender, self-reliant, radiant Helen of nineteen, found themselves looking at each other and then joining hands in an understanding clasp. They were remembering the baffled, tousled "Little Phantom" who had stood on the Keller porch twelve years ago. And now, thanks to Annie's unquenchable courage, wit, and love, she stood on the threshold of college! The battle had been won!

But it hadn't been won. The incredible truth was that Radcliffe didn't want Helen Keller as a student, and made that fact painfully plain. Dean Irwin had signed the certificate of admission, yes, but summoning Helen for an interview, she was very adroit and persuasive in her efforts to dissuade her from entering.

"You have already shown the world you can do the college work by passing your examinations. Wouldn't it be much more desirable to cultivate your writing and do something original than to waste your energy working for a degree?"

For once Helen nearly bowed her head in surrender. "I wanted to go so very, very much," she told Annie with trembling lips. "Was it all foolishness?"

Cornell and the University of Chicago sent her invitations to come to their campuses. But it was Radcliffe Helen had set her face toward. Years later President Woodrow Wilson asked her why. "Because they didn't want me," she told him promptly. Finally, in the autumn of 1900, Radcliffe rather grudgingly opened its doors. The atmosphere was tepid. The freshmen elected her their vice-president, but she had little contact with the girls and not a great deal more with her instructors. The famous Charles Copeland, her instructor in English, made some caustic remarks about her themes. If she would stop trying to pretend she was like everyone else, he said, and write about life as it was for *her*, why then possibly—just possibly, she'd produce something worth his scrutiny. She took him at his word, and began offering him themes dealing with her childhood. "Copey" was stringent in his criticisms, and she wasn't sure whether he thought she had improved or not.

She was in a Latin class one day when someone came and whispered to Annie that Miss Keller had a visitor who wished to see her at once. Surprised and a little alarmed, Helen and Annie went to investigate. Their visitor rose and smiled at them reassuringly.

"Good morning, Miss Sullivan. Will you please tell Miss Keller that I am William Alexander of the staff of the *Ladies' Home Journal,* and that Mr.

Bok, our editor, has sent me here to talk to her?"

Another interview! Even as she interpreted to Helen, Annie was protesting. Miss Keller was extremely busy. She had been called out of a class—

But Mr. Alexander laughed and shook his head. This was definitely not an interview. Mr. Bok had sent him to ask Miss Keller to write the story of her life as a serial for the magazine.

When Annie's amazed fingers interpreted Mr. Alexander's answer Helen sat stunned, but it was her turn to shake her head.

"I am afraid it is out of the question, Mr. Alexander. My college work is all I can manage at present."

Helen had had no experience with editors. When they seek out a story they go forearmed against refusals. "You have already written a considerable part of it in your college themes," Mr. Alexander told her.

Her themes! Annie and Helen clutched one another in breathless astonishment. Outside of Professor Copeland, who could know of themes? "How in the world did you find out about my themes?" demanded Helen. Mr. Alexander waved his hand. "Private information." It was an editor's business to discover such things.

"But seriously, Miss Keller, Mr. Bok wants this story of yours. You have these themes written. Don't you see it will be an easy enough matter to connect them into magazine articles? And of course you will be writing more themes. You have only to bring the story up to date. And if you will sign the contract I have with me, the magazine will pay you three thousand dollars."

Three—thousand—dollars! THREE THOUSAND DOL- LARS? Three—

The words spun dizzily in Helen's brain. Her themes—this famous magazine wanted *her* themes?

And what was Mr. Alexander saying now? "Of course the *Ladies' Home Journal* is buying only the serial rights. The book rights would remain hers."

Dazedly the girl turned toward Annie. "What do you think, Teacher?"

Annie, with her splendid vision of Helen stand- ing among the fine writers of the day coming true before her eyes, said quickly and proudly, "You can do it."

There was a crackling of paper. Annie led Helen to a table and guided the pencil to the spot where she was to sign her first contract.

Helen floated in an ecstatic dream for the next week or two. In her imagination the articles had been speedily written and published—and praised. She confessed later that she touched the peaks of conceit as well as happiness. Annie thrilled at the very thought of the contract. Their tide had really turned. Helen's talents and education were really beginning to pay dividends.

Of course Helen had been writing sketches, themes, even brief stories for several years. She had written entertaining letters almost from the time she possessed a vocabulary. Now she could produce vignettes that her friends told her were vivid, original, witty and poignant. So she sat down to prepare her early themes for the *Ladies' Home Journal* blithely enough. Mr. Alexander had assured her it would be easy. This would be fun. Her fingers tapped out the first installment smoothly. And it read well, too. Mr. Bok was definitely pleased. He published it at once.

Then came the Deluge. To make a smooth, connected manuscript, more material had to be added to her themes. Some of it had been used in her first drafts and then discarded, and her Braille notes had to be ransacked to see if it could be resurrected. Sometimes it could, and then again it had been thrown away and Helen had to rewrite it from memory. Also new sketches had to be written, first in Braille and then on the typewriter. Everything had to be spelled back to her once it was typed. And meanwhile she was forced to keep up with her regular college work.

She fell behind in sending her installments to the *Journal,* and searched her mind frantically to decide what she should say in her next chapter.

Added to this misery telegrams from Philadelphia began flying thick and fast around her head: "We must have next chapter immediately." "There seems to be no connection between pages six and seven. Wire missing part at once."

No wonder Helen and Annie began to feel they were living in a shambles of notes that seemed to deal with everything but the chapter they were working on and they were sure that this was the most muddled and hopeless piece of writing that had ever been undertaken.

In Philadelphia Edward Bok was having his own merry time.

"Young woman," he told Helen years later, "the inhabitants of Dante's *Inferno* had a pleasant time compared to my days while I was waiting for your installments."

And then just as things looked darkest both for the *Journal* and Helen, one of her Wrentham friends strayed in one afternoon while Helen was struggling with a chapter.

"I think I know someone who could help with this," she said thoughtfully. "I think he'd be very good at it, in fact. He's an instructor at Harvard. He writes, and he's on the editorial staff of *Youth's Companion*, too. His name is John Macy. Let me bring him over."

By that time Annie was skeptical about anyone's ability to help. But John Macy came, and listened thoughtfully. He intuitively understood Helen's plight in trying to correlate her notes, memories and written sketches into a series of connected magazine articles, and her desperation at plunging the *Ladies' Home Journal* into such appalling straits. His competent and reassuring attitude about the whole matter inspired Helen to new buoyancy and surprised Annie into relaxing.

Apparently he knew exactly how to go to work, selecting, sorting, suggesting. He did it quietly, with apparent ease, reading aloud, questioning Helen keenly but gently—and when he rose to go at the end of three hours they had a complete installment ready for the *Journal*. To the astonishment of both Helen and Annie, it had been a comparatively painless proceeding.

Mr. Macy paused thoughtfully in the doorway. "I think, Miss Sullivan, you had better teach me this manual alphabet. I will be of much greater assistance to Miss Keller if I can communicate directly with her."

He learned it easily, and was soon using it with dexterity. Mr. Bok was jubilant. He called the manuscript excellent, so Helen could breathe freely again—on that score. When the *Journal* installments were finished, Mr. Wade had them put in Braille and then, for the first time, Helen could read her own story in its entirety.

But there was still work to do. The Century Company wanted to publish it as a book, so Helen used her summer vacation to rewrite the whole story. It seemed to the publishers that, fine and spirited as it was, and outstanding as Helen's writing made it, her autobiography didn't and couldn't, tell her complete story. So John Macy was asked to write a supplemental account. He selected samples of Helen's letters and added essays on her personality, speech, and literary style. Most important of all, he managed to persuade the very reluctant Annie to let him use portions of her letters to Mrs. Hopkins and extracts from her reports to Mr. Anagnos.

So the enlarged version, her first copy of her own book, was placed in Helen's excited hands March 21, 1903. She was an author.

All this while she was at grips with her Radcliffe courses. She might have become an author, but she was still in college—and college wasn't proving the joyous adventure she had thought it would be. She never had all the books she needed, and Annie was obliged to spell into her hand by the hour. There were no recreation periods for them, no relaxed evenings, just spelling and study, study and spelling. Helen developed such violent headaches that it was torture to study, but she never mentioned them to anyone until later.

And then a totally unforeseen disaster loomed. In Helen's senior year Annie began limping so badly that her friends were thoroughly alarmed, and eventually John Macy persuaded her to see an orthopedic surgeon. Annie went reluctantly. When he told her, "Miss Sullivan, you are suffering from a very serious foot condition. Evidently as a child and young girl you were permitted to wear shoes much too small for you," she was not surprised. Nobody at Tewksbury had even considered shoes. She'd worn what she was handed. But when Dr. Goldthwaite added, "It is necessary that you have an immediate operation," Annie answered curtly that it was impossible, at least until Helen was out of college.

Dr. Goldthwaite looked at her gravely. "Miss Sullivan, your health is more important to Helen Keller than her education."

When the remark was relayed to Helen, she said she could have kissed the surgeon on the spot.

Annie still shook her head stubbornly. "We have no money for a hospital."

"Very well," the surgeon smiled at her, "then I will operate in your home"—and he did, on the kitchen table, saving her from permanent lameness. Meanwhile, John Macy read as many of her assignments to Helen as possible, and Leonore Smith, the friend who had introduced John, took her to her classes.

Helen was always mentally breathless now. "The words rush through my hand like hounds in pursuit of a hare they often miss," she lamented.

But in June, 1904, Helen was given her precious degree. No one made special mention of her during commencement. But while the graduates were removing their caps and gowns one girl exclaimed indignantly, "Miss Sullivan should have received a degree as well as Helen!"

Nobody noticed them as they slipped away from Radcliffe for the last time, and neither of them felt like talking as they took the street car for Lake Wollomonapoag.

But they carried with them the sheepskin which testified that Helen Adams Keller had graduated *cum laude,* excelling in English literature.

And her four years at Radcliffe had been the cause of three events which made indelible impressions on both Helen Keller's and Annie Sullivan's lives:

Because Helen Keller went to Radcliffe she had written themes; because Edward Bok heard of the themes she wrote the *Story of My Life;* because she had needed help with the book, John Macy had come into their lives.

And John Macy had fallen in love with Annie.

CHAPTER · 18

Trio
At
Wrentham

ANNIE HERSELF WAS BEWILDERED and incredulous. She had never been in a position to make even casual friends of her own. The people she met were always interested mainly in Helen; and even if she'd had the opportunity, there would have been no time. She had been too breathlessly busy keeping pace with Helen's education. Years ago Annie had linked her life with Helen's, and that was that. Oh, there were several opportunities to leave, two or three of them financially tempting, but she had brushed them aside. In her heart she believed she and Helen belonged together.

She had liked John Macy, the young teacher from

Harvard from the start—first for the understanding and valuable help he had given Helen with her book, but after that for himself. His tastes and his philosophy appealed to her. He had a vigorous mind and delightful humor, but perhaps what appealed to her most was the force of his quiet gentleness. Annie could be tense, combative and defensive—she suffered terribly from a sense of inferiority—but somehow John Macy unraveled all the tangled skeins in her just as he had unraveled them in Helen's manuscript. This was new to Annie.

But when John began talking of loving her, and of marriage—then she really was startled. To think of anyone's loving her—wanting her—thinking her more important than Helen! She could only stare at John Macy unbelievingly. Annie Sullivan had had many experiences. This one she had never expected.

In the months that followed she tried to marshal all her arguments against marriage. She didn't think she was fit for it temperamentally. She was older than John. Yes; he admitted that fact, but it didn't disturb him. She and Helen had just bought a house in Wrentham. Her home must always be Helen's, and marriage wouldn't alter her love or care for the girl. Yes, John understood that. There was something else, a thought that tortured her sometimes—the fear of possible blindness.

At that John Macy kissed her gravely. "We will face that together, Anne."

"Anne." He had transformed her from plain Annie

to the more fashionable Anne. Even with her name he was different.

It was certainly a new life they were starting. To begin with, there was the new house in Wrentham. Annie had never lived in a house she could call her own before, and Helen had spent very little time in Tuscumbia since she was nine.

Helen and Annie had sold some stock given to them years ago by John Spaulding, and had bought a friendly farmhouse surrounded by seven rambling acres, mostly overgrown with weeds.

"Dear Mr. Spaulding seems very near to us today," Helen said on the lovely June day they took possession.

Wrentham had everything. It was only twenty-six miles from Boston, in the clean, fragrant country they both loved. There were winding, rambling, tree-shaded little roads, and real woods to be explored, and lakes for boats and swimming—and the seven acres for a farm and gardens. The house had a comfortable, hospitable feeling. Annie had two pantries and a dairy thrown into one room for Helen's study, and a long balcony built outside her bedroom, so she could enjoy being outdoors by herself.

Here, in her first home, she tried to chart her future. Was she to accept John Macy's love and companionship and join her life to his, or devote herself fully to Helen for the rest of her days?

Once she told Helen decisively, "I will never marry anyone." And Helen cried out, "Oh, Teacher,

if you love John and let him go, I will feel like a
hideous accident."

Even after they had announced their engagement
and set the day, Annie changed her mind so often
that John Macy laughingly threatened to have "Subject to change without notice," engraved on the
wedding invitations.

But finally, on a May morning a year after Helen
had graduated, Annie stood in her room at Wrentham and let Mrs. Hopkins dress her as that motherly soul had dressed her for her graduation from
Perkins.

"My, oh, my! Oh, my, my alive!" Mrs. Hopkins
kept repeating under her breath as her fingers trembled over the bridal dress. She remembered other
days in Annie's life—the day she had first seen her,
a restless, uncertain girl with a defiant face; and
and then the day she had whirled into Mrs. Hopkins' arms, waving Mr. Anagnos' letter and the one
from Captain Keller. And now her Annie was a
bride, and the famous Dr. Edward Everett Hale
was waiting to perform the ceremony.

And so on May 2, 1905, in the presence of Kate
Keller, John Hitz, Sophia Hopkins, and Leonore
Smith (who had brought bride and groom together)
and the Macy family, and with Helen as her only
attendant, Annie Sullivan became Anne Macy.

Everyone rejoiced. Mrs. Keller thought John Macy
was exactly the sort of person Annie needed. "For

so many years you've been cut off from everything human and natural," she exclaimed. "Now you will have someone to shield you and love you." Dr. Bell and Dr. Hale approved too. Dr. Hale told Helen she had gained a brother. Mark Twain summoned the trio for a visit, and he admired John Macy.

Wrentham was a happy place the first years of the Macy marriage. Freed from the strain and grind of Helen's education, and with her husband trying his best to prevent further abuse of her eyes, Annie regained her natural buoyancy and her scintillating personality flashed out. She proved herself a "born cook," and she was an eager hostess. Mrs. Keller was invited to be at Wrentham for months at a time. So was Mrs. Hopkins. Mr. Hitz spent weeks with them in the summer, and the family loved them all. The Macy latchstring was always out, perhaps especially for Mr. Hitz, who had always considered Annie and Helen his foster daughters, keeping a close watch over them all the while Helen was growing up. Annie called him *"Mon père,"* and Helen called him *"Pflegevater."* And it was Mr. Hitz who showed Helen a path which neither of the Macys could follow when he gave her a Braille copy of Swedenborg's *Heaven and Hell.*

Helen had been taught a doctrine of love by Phillips Brooks as a child, but in her college days she had become bewildered and dissatisfied by the conflict between creeds and science. She opened

233

Heaven and Hell because it was a book and she read everything she could touch. Before she finished it she had found her faith. Radiant, she rushed to pour her discovery into Annie's ears, but in this one thing neither of the Macys could give her any sympathy. They had no religion at all.

"You know perfectly well you are talking moonshine," Annie told her.

But Helen had found her religion, a religion that has enriched her life ever since, and sensing her conviction and joy in it the Macys went out of their way to find and read everything they could on the subject.

When they had bought the farmhouse, Helen had been enchanted.

"Now we will have a farm like Father's," she declared, "with wonderful trees, and crops and marvelous gardens."

One thing she forgot. In Tuscumbia her father had the help of several Negro workers. She and Annie had no money for farm hands, and gardening required more sight than Annie possessed. And literary John Macy wasn't exactly farmer material.

Well, then, they could have animals. They began to read the advertisements in the *Boston Transcript*. There was one that actually brought tears to Helen's eyes. A Boston woman who owned a great Dane must go abroad and leave her wonderful pet. If only someone who really loved and understood animals would offer Nimrod a good home she would give him away for seventy-five dollars. Why, Wrentham would be ideal. They wrote Nimrod's owner at once, and John Macy went to fetch him. He was wearing a peculiar look when he returned. Helen's hands explored the dog eagerly. She had never encountered such an immense dog.

"Dog?" said John Macy. "He is more like a young elephant to me. I suggest we leave him out here on the porch until we find out about his upbringing."

Both Annie and Helen were indignant. How could he think of being so cruel? The door was flung open. Nimrod was to feel at home. Nimrod crashed in, upsetting a table and a lamp on his way. Bounding on into the dining room, he charged the table and knocked Mr. Macy's supper and the dishes all over the room. He was finally captured and shut in the barn, and the Macy relations were strained that evening.

The next day Nimrod was released to roam the field—a safe pastime. But then it was discovered that he was eating stones. Annie sent for the state veterinarian. The doctor's report was disconcerting. "This dog has no teeth, and very little sight. He is at the stage where the safest thing is to put him to sleep. His former owner was probably too tenderhearted to do it. But I think you had better give me permission." Annie and Helen were staggered and shocked—but it seemed wisest.

Still the innocents not only had hopes, but trust in the *Transcript's* advertisements. The next time they settled on a horse, proclaimed "fearless, spirited, and fit for a lady to ride or drive." He was lovely to look at, and Helen named him Whitefoot on the spot. They paid cash, and a boy rode him to Wrentham, but neglected to tell the Macys he'd been thrown three times on the way. The next morning John hitched him to a light carriage, but they hadn't left the driveway when Whitefoot showed signs of stubbornness. John got out to investigate, and at that timely moment a car passed. Whitefoot jumped, and lunged across the lawn and out the gate into the road, smashing the carriage to kindling against a stone post on his way. It was two days before he was found and the veterinarian pronounced him crazy.

Despite their mischances with animals and farming, John Macy gave Annie the understanding and help she needed, and made a perfect literary companion for Helen. He was the best critic and advisor she ever had, and she really reveled in his appraisals of her work. He introduced her to all the new books as they came out, reading them into her hand, or if it was feasible, arranging to have them done in Braille. And he talked to her just as he would have talked to anyone else. Helen was a little amused sometimes. She said he "put his words together as carefully as though he was writing a novel," but she was enthralled at the brilliance of his conversation and listened eagerly as he talked to her about politics, Socialist leaders (he was becoming an ardent Socialist), world affairs, and literature. And she was both delighted and grateful at the way he managed to include her in everyday happenings.

He was thoughtful of her in other ways, too. He strung wires from the house to the woods so that Helen might walk in freedom by herself. They extended a quarter of a mile, marking the longest walk alone she has ever been able to take. Once when she was working on a manuscript and hadn't been able to finish her copy, he sat up all night, typing forty pages so that it might reach the publisher on time.

They were both working very hard at writing. Helen was doing a series of articles for the *Century Magazine,* and John Macy was writing the essays that would put him in the top rank of American critics, continuing his editorial work for the *Youth's Companion,* and writing a biography of Edgar Allan Poe. Helen did her one long poem, "Song of the Stone Wall," and her next book, *The World I Live In.* After the publication of *The Story of My Life,* there had been ridiculous complaints that a deaf-blind girl couldn't know half the things she wrote about, and Helen was trying to explain in this new book how she substituted touch, vibratory sense, taste and smell for sight and hearing. How, for example, she recognized her friends by their perfume or tobacco odor; how, from vibrations, she knew whether a carpenter was using a plane, a saw, or a hammer; how she knew gay music from sad, and how, in a hotel dining room she had once been fascinated and baffled by discords in the vibrations she was "hearing" with her feet. Eventually she discovered that a band was playing, and she felt the music waves along the floor. At the same time two waiters were making their rounds, but one "walked in time to the music, graceful and light, and the other rushed from table to table to the beat of some discord in his own mind."

And once, when she and Dr. Bell were walking in the rain he had stopped, and made her touch a young oak tree, "and she felt a delicate murmur—a silvery whisper as if the leaves were telling each other a lot of little things."

Perhaps the loveliest vibratory experience she ever had came at Wrentham one May day, when she was alone on her balcony. At the south end grew a wonderful wisteria vine that would curl its gently clinging fingers around hers when she touched it. The day was bewitching with its fragrance of apple blossoms, and suddenly, as Helen stood with her hand on the railing, she felt a vibration utterly new to her. The pulsations were rhythmical, and repeated over and over. Suddenly they stopped, and she felt the wisteria against her cheek. She knew a bird was swaying the vine, and then he was back on the rail. She didn't dare move or call, but suddenly Annie was touching her quietly by reaching her hand out the window.

"It's a whippoorwill," she spelled. "He's standing on the corner post close to you. You could touch him."

Now that she knew what the bird was, Helen could detect the beat of his call: "Whippoorwill! Whippoorwill! Whippoorwill!"

"His lady love is answering him from the apple tree," Annie's fingers told her. "Now they are singing a duet."

Helen stood holding the precious moment as long as she could, but the railing finally ceased to vibrate, and Annie gave her the information, "They are together in the apple tree, singing their hearts out in a billow of pink-and-white blossoms."

That was like Annie—and John Macy, too—to give Helen intimate color details no one else would have thought of telling a blind girl.

In 1906 Helen had her first definite assignment of public work for the blind. She was appointed to the Massachusetts Commission for the Blind. She was disappointed and indignant that the appointment hadn't gone to Annie, but consoled because, as she reminded herself, Annie would go everywhere with her.

From then on she was assailed on all sides by

people who thought Helen Keller must be an authority on all problems of the blind, and a wonder-worker who knew how to solve them all. Letters upon letters poured in upon her. Wrentham became a clearing-house for the difficulties of the blind everywhere. She was begged for aid for the blind of all ages, asked for articles or personal appearances. People clamored at her door for advice. And suddenly Helen was aghast to find how little she did know about blindness or the blind—and how much she would have to know if she was to be of any real help. She set herself to learn, and that took work—not only answering the letters, but studying and reading. And once again Annie was taxing her eyes to their limits, only this time John Macy was in on it too, helping with the research, sorting, assembling, reading books and pamphlets not only in English, but in French and German as well.

It was John Macy who said rather grimly, "Helen Keller has become an institution rather than a person."

Meanwhile John Macy was becoming a more and more ardent Socialist. He brought Socialist leaders like Joe Ettor and Arturo Giovannitti home. Annie was skeptical at first about this pattern for a bright, fine new world, but after she'd read *New Worlds For Old,* by H. G. Wells, and listened to John explain his views, Helen was a fervent convert, and two or three years later, disgusted at the brutality with which a strike by the textile workers at Lawrence, Massachusetts, was handled by the authorities, Annie joined them.

No one cared what John and Anne Macy believed, but when Helen proclaimed herself a Socialist and wrote articles about Socialism, there was a great outcry from the newspapers. Helen Keller, the pure, sweet, innocent girl, associating with such human rubbish. How terrible of those awful Macys to mislead her into the paths of Socialism. In vain Helen protested that she had studied political economics, and that she read, thought and decided things for herself.

In 1912 Schenectady, New York, focused attention on itself by electing the first Socialist mayor, George Richard Lunn. Mayor Lunn asked John Macy to be his secretary, and offered Helen a place on the Board of Welfare. John Macy accepted with delight but Helen refused. She had resigned from the Massachusetts Commission for the Blind because she couldn't readily go from place to place gathering firsthand information, and the slowness with which the proceedings had to be communicated to her prevented her from taking the rapid-fire part she should in the meetings, so she felt she had no place on boards. Also, for the first time since her Wright-Humanson days, she was seriously trying to improve and strengthen her voice, and Charles White, her teacher, was coming to Wrentham three times a week. But the really important reason both she and Annie had for not wanting to go to a strange city was Annie's health. She was hounded by some obscure illness that was depleting her strength.

In the end John Macy went to Schenectady alone, and for four months Annie and Helen carried on at Wrentham alone. Then in September their world crashed in. Annie was suddenly hurried to the hospital for a serious operation. John resigned his position and returned home. Leonore Smith came and carried Helen away to her Washington home.

For perhaps the first time in her life Helen was in the grip of a horrible, paralyzing fear. She carried with her the memory of Annie's hand too weak to spell words of farewell. And she knew the doctors had doubts as to whether Annie would recover. She was suddenly sickeningly aware of what a burden she really was.

"I am a perpetual stumbling block, a handicap, a hindrance," she cried in despair, "a hanger-on, an upsetter of plans, a tremendous burden!"

Leonore Smith tried to comfort her, but for the time being Helen was beyond comfort. She wrote John Macy, "Do tell me promptly . . . ANYTHING that happens."

One thing that acutely distressed Helen was her own utter helplessness in the strange house. Many deaf-blind people have an almost uncanny ability to tell distance and direction. Helen never had it. In a strange place she was lost.

But the bulletins from Wrentham became optimistic, and when a joyful Helen was permitted to return home she found Annie weak, but well on the road to recovery.

CHAPTER · 19

Rugged
Roads

OF COURSE, THE DOCTORS HAD CAUTIONED Annie that she must be extremely careful of herself for a year. But Annie was in no position to be careful. There were urgent reasons why she and Helen had to have an income outside of Helen's writing, and an opening had come for a lecture tour. Helen plunged once more into her lessons with Mr. White, and in less than four months she and Annie were standing on a platform in Montclair, New Jersey, trying to infuse courage in each other for their first lecture.

"Terror invaded my flesh," Helen said afterward, "my mind froze. I kept repeating, What shall I do? What shall I do?" And then she prayed, Oh, God, let me pour out my voice freely.

But she stood there silent and shuddering. At

last she felt a sound emerge from her throat. It felt like an explosion. She was told afterward it was the faintest whisper. Sometimes her voice went soaring upward, and she knew that meant a squeak. When she tried to force it down "it fell about me like loose bricks." Once off the platform she surrendered to a storm of tears, sobbing, "Oh, it is too difficult. I can never help the blind." She would never step on a platform again.

But her audience thought differently. They crowded around with sincere praise and interest. And Helen gathered the shreds of her courage and made another appearance and then another. The speaking was never easy, but then, nothing that Helen had ever accomplished had been particularly easy for her.

She had two motives for wanting to make good at this. One was her conviction that her life work would be for the blind—and she could speak from experience on that subject—and the other was the very real need of an income. She had found, to her disappointment and dismay, that she could not support herself on what she earned by writing, and John Macy's income wouldn't care for the three of them. Besides, there was a growing tension between Annie and her husband. Their marriage had always been a combination of two brilliant, unpredictable personalities. There were beginning to be symptoms that it would not last. A lecture bureau offered

Helen and Annie an engagement. Despite Annie's slender strength it seemed best to take it. They went on tour.

Helen never enjoyed the hotels, most of which were poor, but she did like the train trips, the smooth motion, and the anticipation of success in the next city.

She would tell how she was educated, and she and Annie would give a demonstration of the finger alphabet and lip reading; Helen would speak of the needs of the blind, and Annie would repeat the sentences after her, and then there would be questions. Helen would put on what she called her "Job-like expression," and patiently answer them all:

"No, I do not play the piano or sing. . . . Yes, I know day is not night. . . . No, I am not always joyful. . . . Yes, fire burns blind people. . . . Yes, we like to eat when we are hungry."

Whenever she could, she visited schools for the blind or the deaf. But she was growing more and more worried about Annie. Sometimes her teacher trembled so that Helen wondered if she would finish the performance on her feet. But still Annie would go on. Until a day in Bath, Maine. Feverish, exhausted and shaking, Annie fell into her hotel bed one night and dropped into a troubled sleep. She woke late in the morning to find a frightened Helen leaning over her.

"Teacher—Teacher, what is it? Are you ill?"

Annie groped for Helen's hand and tried to spell

reassurances, but found that she could not. She could only moan and shiver with the chills that shook her. Somehow Helen realized that she was desperately ill, and terror gripped iron fingers around her.

"What shall I do?" she sobbed. "What can I do? Help me to get help for Teacher, oh, please, dear God, help of the helpless—help me now."

Her deafness made it impossible for her to use the room telephone; she could not find her way downstairs. Fright made her voice so tight she couldn't call for help. Finally the hotel attendant came, and a doctor was called. Several days later the hotel manager put them on a train for Boston.

Helen knew then what she had to do. Three years before, Andrew Carnegie had offered her a life pension and she had proudly refused. Back in Wrentham, Helen fought down her pride and humbly wrote him, confessing her difficulties and her helplessness to meet them. It was the hardest thing she ever did. Back came a check, and the most heart-soothing letter the generous Scot ever wrote:

There are a few great souls who can rise to the height of allowing others to do for them what they would like to do for others. So you have risen.

Even with Mr. Carnegie's aid, the lectures went on. But by now Mrs. Keller had joined them. She shared her daughter's love of travel, but with Annie's waning health and worsening sight the tours were torture. Still she kept on. The audiences had eyes only for Helen—or so they thought—but without Annie's skillful translations of her speech and her fascinating demonstrations of how Helen had been taught the audiences probably would have lost interest. Annie had a marvelous speaking voice and a delightful stage presence.

Sometimes the tours were spiced with odd incidents. Once their train entered a flooded area in Texas, where Helen could actually feel the water slapping angry fingers against the coach windows and every now and then there would be a jar as they hit a dead cow or uprooted tree.

And then there was the time when they left Salt Lake City on a bitterly cold day, wearing furs. In the middle of the night they were awakened by a violent commotion. Their train had jumped the tracks. Luckily they were not hurt. They were transferred to a rickety train, and clattered on their uncomfortable way to Los Angeles. By the time they reached the city the three fur-clad women felt as though they'd been in a steam-house.

The year 1914 was a bitter one. John Macy left Annie.

"He had many reasons for wanting to leave us," Helen said sadly. And perhaps he did. Helen's friends (aside from Andrew Carnegie) had withdrawn most of their financial support after Annie's marriage, and financially the Wrentham household was on decidedly shaky ground. Annie was eleven years older than John Macy, and although she had been fair in her warning that Helen would always come first with her, he couldn't possibly have known that Helen would become, as he himself put it, "an institution"—an institution that would be like a juggernaut engulfing home and personal life.

There never was a divorce. He simply stepped out of Annie's life, and when he went he took her exuberant spirit and lightness of step with him. It was a time of great suffering for Annie, and only a little less so for Helen.

One bright thing 1914 did bring them, however, was a new member of their household. Much as Mrs. Keller enjoyed the tours, it was obvious that she couldn't handle all the details of Helen's growing work for the blind, and Annie's sight, especially since her personal distress, was becoming more and more unpredictable. Helen needed a secretary. Polly Thomson was a fresh, spirited girl just over from Scotland, seeking a position in America. She knew absolutely nothing about the blind—and in fact she had never heard of Helen Keller. But she needed a job, and Helen needed a secretary.

Polly wasn't in the least literary, but she was practical. She could balance a checkbook, arrange a day's schedule, say "No," to the doorbell and the telephone: handle persistent callers with polite compliments, easing them out of the door at the same time. She could manage Helen's always-increasing correspondence with cheery dispatch. She was strong and vigorous, but she had a quality of sure understanding for the world of the handicapped which the strong and normal person doesn't always possess. She was soon adept at Helen's finger speech, and cut herself a permanent niche in both Annie's and Helen's hearts.

For twenty-four years their friends had been asking, "What would Helen do without Annie?" Now they wondered, "What would either of them do without Polly?"

Perhaps Helen answered that when she said, "Had it not been for her devotion, adaptability and willingness to give up every individual pleasure we should long ago have found it necessary to retire into complete isolation."

She brought a personality into their two lives that was as reviving as a sea-breeze. It refreshed and stimulated Helen and steadied and strengthened Annie.

John Macy's going had closed one door in their lives. In the same year Polly Thomson opened another onto new horizons wider and more varied than they had ever suspected they would find.

CHAPTER · 20

Curtain Fall
For
Teacher

Annie had been more or less ill for some time but she'd refused to acknowledge the fact. Polly had wanted to visit her family in Scotland for a few weeks in the summer, and who could refuse her after two years? Annie had no family to call her own, but she did know what it was like to work without respite. And Helen had a Chautauqua circuit tour scheduled at the same time, so Annie ignored the slight pain in her side and other warnings, and accompanied her. This time the burden hadn't fallen completely upon her shoulders. Helen had a substitute secretary, a newspaper man from Boston recommended by John Macy. Helen enjoyed him, and Annie thought him a fine person. Somehow she managed to weather the Chautauqua business, but once back in Wrentham the pain in her side grew so breath-taking that she had to surrender to it. Annie had pleurisy—a desperate attack. Polly returned, but Annie hadn't recovered. Her cough and fever remained. A curious cough. Far back in her unhappy childhood she had known two people to cough that way. Her mother and her brother Jimmie. Annie wasn't too surprised at the doctor's verdict. He suspected tuberculosis. She must go to Lake Placid at once.

Helen was shocked and stunned. Her mother, who had come from Alabama to care for the Wrentham household, said her face could have been used for a classic mask of grief.

And now it was time for Annie to go. Polly had brought her coat, and Annie slowly lifted her tired arms and obediently slid them into the sleeves. She was glad Polly was going with her.

Helen came close to her and took her arm and together they walked slowly to the car. They did not dare to kiss, but there were a few hurriedly-spelled words, and then a convulsive clasping of hands. And Helen wrote to her the next day, "I don't know how I stood the pain of having you go. As we walked to the car I was suddenly overwhelmed with nameless dread."

During the days of Annie's desperate illness Helen had been overwhelmed by a sense of aloneness.

Only two people, Teacher and John Macy, had ever succeeded in freeing her completely from her feeling of isolation. John Macy was gone and Teacher . . . was some grim destiny sweeping her away too? Helen was engulfed in such a torrent of utter desolation that she couldn't read, write, or even think. For the first time in her life she felt "that it was folly" for her to be alive.

And then, one evening as she sat in her study, she felt the door open. She knew it was the young newspaperman-secretary. And she held out her hands to him.

He sat down and took her hand. For a long time he comforted her just by his clasp. And then he began talking to her. She was astounded. Like Annie before her, she had never thought this kind of love could be for her. She thought it was "like a beautiful flower I must not touch." The young man thought differently. She was brave and sweet and good. He loved her.

She listened trembling. As the days went by they walked in the autumn woods, and read and talked. Even through her concern for Teacher her happiness mounted. They planned together. And all his plans included Teacher. But he loved Helen. When he asked her to marry him she consented.

She knew it was right. Years ago Dr. Bell had talked to her of a time when a young man would come knocking at the door of her heart, and he bade her not to hesitate because of her handicaps. Since

neither her blindness or her deafness was inherited
she could not transmit it. She had said then that she
thought marrying her would be "like marrying a
statue," and she never anticipated it. But love had
come. And she returned it.

But they both agreed that silence would be best
for a while. Teacher must be the first to hear, and
she was too ill to be told just then. And Mrs. Keller
was too busy and upset. And then, one day they
went to the length of applying for a marriage license, and Helen was aquiver with joy.

"I am going to tell Mother and Teacher everything tomorrow," she said when they parted.

Full of her joyous plans, Helen was dressing the
next morning when her mother rushed into her
room, in a hot storm of indignation.

"What is the meaning of this? The morning papers
are full of a dreadful story. What have you been
doing? Tell me! Tell me!" Her fingers shook as she
spelled out her angry questions. "Are you engaged
to him? Did you really get a license as this paper
says you did?"

Some curious reporter roaming the country for
news had found the application.

Under her mother's angry tirade, sensing her hostility, Helen's wits fled. She did what she always
bitterly repented of doing. She lied. She told her
mother she knew nothing about it. She kept on
denying it. For the first and perhaps the only time
in her life she betrayed "the beautiful truth" as well

as someone who loved her. Mrs. Keller furiously forbade the young man the house. He sent Helen a Braille note, telling her where he would be, begging her to write. They never saw each other again. Mrs. Keller warned Helen not to mention the affair to Teacher. They would go South as soon as Teacher could travel. But when the Kellers did turn their faces toward Alabama, Annie had already been sentenced to Lake Placid.

The next months were miserable for Helen, first because of her denial of the one who had offered her his life and love, and second because of the terror of Teacher's illness. Furthermore she was in a strange house, not her childhood home in Tuscumbia, but her sister's home in Montgomery. Mildred was Mrs. Warren Tyson, now.

Meanwhile at Lake Placid Annie, whose illness had been diagnosed as tuberculosis, was as miserable as a human being could be. She had been told to "lie still, relax, and enjoy the cold." Annie hated being still. She hated being cold. She hated being ill. Then she discovered a short item in the *New York Times* extolling the glories of Puerto Rico.

"Polly," said Annie with sudden decision, "we are going to Puerto Rico. I am tired of being cooped up here with these sick, stodgy people." She smiled for the first time in weeks. "Please pack our things—now!"

And despite the doctors' protests and forebodings they went, sailing for eleven days out of the wintry, leaden weather which had chilled her so much to a sun-warmed ocean where an island of flowers lay in a sea of violet waters. Annie wrote Helen she had to pinch herself to be sure it was there—and that she was there as well.

There were hundreds of things she wanted to tell Helen directly, and she was dismayed to discover she'd forgotten her Braille, not having used it in twenty years. Even after Helen sent her the alphabet, she was annoyed to find what truly hard work writing a Braille letter was.

"You have no idea," she wrote Helen, "what a job it is for me. The stiletto is so awkward in my hand, it feels like punching a hole in the universe with a toe."

But then, so great was her need to pour the glory and delight of this amazing place and her own ecstasy in it into Helen's eager hands, that she pricked out long letters, each one mounting in rhapsody.

One can't help being happy here, Helen—happy and idle and aimless and pagan—all the sins we are warned against. I go to bed every night soaked with sunshine and orange blossoms. . . . We sit on the porch every evening and watch the sunset melt from one vivid color to another—rose, asphodel, violet, then deep purple. Polly and I hold our breath as the stars come out of the sky—they hang low in the heavens like lamps of many colors—and myriads of fireflies come out in the grass and twinkle in the dark trees.

In nearly every letter she begged Helen and her mother to come to Puerto Rico. There was no use to worry, fret or wonder about the future. Somehow it seemed impossible to do any of these things down here. All she had to do was rest and be comfortable and "soak up the sunshine."

Her letters were an absolute delight to Helen. She told Annie:

You'd laugh to hear how everybody urges me to give them the news. I pretend to grumble about making out your Braille, because I am selfish enough to want to read it all through myself first.

In one of her letters Helen had a piece of real drama to offer. For some reason she had lain awake one night vaguely conscious of a slight steamy smell, but it was a familiar odor, and she thought nothing of it until suddenly she was aware of burning tar and wood! She sprang up and darted into her mother's room. Kate Keller went to investigate and found a flame six feet high! The fire had started directly under Helen's bed, and she had discovered it just in time to save herself and indeed the whole house!

"It seems as if I could never sleep again without putting my face close to the floor and hunting all over for a hidden spark," she confessed.

War was drawing nearer to the United States. She

had a terror of Teacher's sailing home through submarine-infested waters, and begged her to come quickly. Annie was feeling so happy and so perfectly well in her "Joy Isle" that she was more loath to leave than Helen could know. But she capitulated. "I know you still need me," she told Helen, and she and Polly came home in April. The Kellers met them at the dock in New York, and the four women went on to Wrentham on the sad errand of dismantling the house and selling it, and when that was over Annie was finally persuaded to go back to the Lake Placid doctors for a check-up. They greeted her with smiles.

"Well, Mrs. Macy," one doctor told her cheerily, "we have good news for you." He rubbed his hands. "Very good news indeed!"

"You mean," Annie asked with bated breath, "that my case is checked?"

"Oh, no, no, not that at all," the doctor shook his head. "I mean—that you never had tuberculosis. You see," he finished suavely, "your laboratory reports got mixed with another patient's."

The First World War hurt Helen almost as cruelly as though she had lived in the midst of it. She felt that both Christianity and civilization had been betrayed. And when she made over the proceeds of the German edition of *The Story Of My Life* for the benefit of blinded German soldiers, an outcry arose that she was pro-German. The only reason that French blind soldiers did not benefit was because there wasn't a French edition.

258

She and Annie made the rounds of hospitals to visit blinded soldiers and sailors. "Gee," said one young man, "I used to read about you in school. But I never thought I'd be—blind—myself!"

They would go away shaken and dismayed. Helen could tell the men that life had not ended. She told them how much they could still do. She even danced with them. But she had no adequate words of comfort.

"I have never known an abrupt, soul-shaking plunge into blindness," she mourned. "I've never had to put my life together again in the dark."

Early in 1918 someone in Hollywood had a flash of inspiration: Helen Keller's life would make a wonderful movie. The idea was presented to Helen in glowing terms. Here was a glorious opportunity to win friends and funds for the blind, and enough money to make Annie's future secure. Helen was concerned about that. Her own pension and most of their income would cease at her death, and with John Macy gone what would become of Annie if she chanced to survive Helen?

Besides, making a movie would be an adventure. And for once in her life Helen's lack of a normal voice wouldn't matter—movies were silent affairs in 1918.

The finished spectacle resembled a circus spectacle more than Helen's life. It was no wonder it flopped.

But there were other ventures that were distinctly

worth while—their vaudeville appearances, for example. Many people were shocked and distressed that Helen Keller, of all people, should demean herself by appearing in vaudeville. But her vaudeville tours won her many lasting friends, and spread the knowledge of what deaf-blind people could accomplish and how they could be helped far more effectively than her lectures ever had—and at a much better salary.

At first everyone had been a little nervous. This was altogether different from the lecture tours. Their lecture audiences had been well-bred, courteous, earnest people. Vaudeville audiences could be rowdy, disturbing, and merciless to performers who failed to meet their standards. How would they react to a deaf-blind star and her teacher? Even Helen and Annie wondered and dreaded the ordeal of their first performances.

Their dread was groundless. Both of them always had magnetic stage personalities. "You always tell Helen's story as if you were telling it for the first time," people marveled; and the New York *Sun-and-Herald* said that "within two minutes the most critical and cynical audience in the world was Helen's."

Helen always felt the friendly enthusiasm of the audiences. She loved it, and was amused when she wore cerise, which was very becoming, or some other color, and received protests: her audience wanted her to wear white. Polly found vaudeville life an adventure too, but poor Annie loathed it. She walked on half-ill most of the time, the spotlights tortured her eyes, and her voice failed.

So, despite the fact that for the first time in their lives they were earning an exceptionally good salary, after four years they retreated to their new home in Forest Hills. But their destinies never led them along quiet, easy roads. By 1922 they had plunged headlong into work for the newly-founded American Foundation for the Blind, and Helen and Annie were taking an active part in its campaigns for the prevention of blindness, the education and employment of the blind, the use of the Talking Book, and perhaps most of all the adoption of one standard system of Braille. This last was especially close to Helen's heart.

Ridiculous as it seems, there were five different sets of alphabets for the blind. There were two types of embossed letters: Boston Line type, devised by Dr. Howe, and the Moon type. Neither of these was easy to read, and then couldn't be written. Then there were three systems of Braille: New York Point, American and English. "Be" in English Braille would be "is" in New York Point and "to" in American. In order to read all books available in raised print a blind person had to know all five.

No wonder Helen cried out, "A plague on all these types and systems! For my part, I wish nothing had ever been invented except English Braille."

She and Annie campaigned vigorously for one

system. And in 1932 English Braille became the standard system. Ironically despite its name, it is practically letter-for-letter the point system Louis Braille devised in 1829. It took the world one hundred and three years to recognize its superiority and adopt it as the universal alphabet for the blind.

In between campaigns Helen managed to write two more books—*My Religion,* and the second part of her autobiography, *Midstream.* By this time Annie's sight had become so dim that she could read only with the help of double-lens glasses—like small telescopes. The very weight of them on her face made it impossible to wear them for more than brief periods. Hearing of this and other difficulties, Helen's publisher, Mr. Doubleday, sent one of the Doubleday staff, Nella Braddy, to Forest Hills to help Helen with her books. Nella became the close friend of the three women, and finally grew so impressed with Teacher's life that she wrote a book of her own, *Anne Sullivan Macy, the Story Behind Helen Keller.*

And not until then did Helen hear the story of Annie's miserable life at Tewksbury.

Several times Helen, Annie, and Polly went abroad, trying to do it incognito, but everywhere they went they were recognized, welcomed, entertained, and asked to speak.

Annie loved England, France, and Scotland. But Ireland depressed her. "No one smiles." It was in Scotland that a cablegram was handed her. John

Macy was dead. She let the paper flutter from her hand.

Annie had been an exceptionally vigorous and active woman until mid-life. She always said neither she nor Helen could have accomplished what they did without the glorious vitality both possessed. She hated the thoughts of illness, weakness, and blindness. And now they were all closing in on her. Still her courage carried her on until October of 1936. She had always claimed she was without religion. "There is a quirk in my mind against the word immortality," she had told Helen. But now she said to her, "I feel that I am at peace, lying at the feet of God."

And a few days later, on the twentieth of October, she had lapsed into a merciful coma from which even Helen's loving hand could not summon her.

CHAPTER · 21

To
Live
Again

"THE DEEPEST SORROW knows no time—it is like an eternal night," wrote Helen in her Journal some ten days later.

She and Polly had sailed for Scotland in answer to a cabled invitation from Polly's minister brother in Bothwell. Teacher's ashes had been placed in the National Cathedral in Washington. Now it was time to turn away from the scene of suffering and parting and bitter loss and begin the climb back to hope, and service, and happiness—to live again. The Bothwell manse, brimming over with the antics of four children and several dogs, together with the sure understanding and gentleness she knew Bert and Isobel Thomson possessed, was a fine place to go to gain the first footholds for that climb. It was good for them both to go—good for Polly, who had borne the brunt of the long siege of nursing and responsibility, and for Helen, who acknowledged that it would have been next to impossible to recover her mental equilibrium in the sorrowful house at Forest Hills. Only, when one was so numbed, so completely empty, could one ever feel whole again?

The Thomson manse was a good place to be, and although neither Helen nor Polly realized it, their "living again" probably began even before the minister drove into the driveway; it began when the eldest Thomson son, David, flung open the manse door in welcome, and the other children tumbled out of the house to greet them. There was a cheerful open fire, and hot tea waiting for them, but there was something more comforting in the room even than warmth; it was as though loving, understanding hands were stretched out to them.

For over a month Helen seemed to be living in a strange, divided state. Part of her read and wrote, cheered and steadied Polly who was plunged into an abyss of grief herself. She joined in the Thomson family's preparations for Christmas, taking her turn at stirring the great plum pudding, laughing at the "plump, beribboned, besprigged parcels which sit on my table exchanging compliments of the season

265

with my Braille manuscripts and typewriter," or climbing a stepladder to "look at the festoons stretched across the hall."

The two younger Thomson boys, fourteen-year-old Robert and twelve-year-old John, appointed themselves her guardians, and made very sure there was nothing for her to stumble over, or if there was anything interesting or exciting going on, they would run to tell her.

David brought his radio to have her touch the diaphragm and "listen" to Big Ben, and the others were always eagerly calling her attention to something special.

It seemed to Helen that one part of her laughed and talked with the Thomson family, while another part was "wrapped in a tempest of grief."

But not for nothing had Teacher passed her creed of loving service on to Helen. Three days after Christmas Helen was writing in her journal:

Today my head is buzzing with a letter which seems like the call of destiny. . . . Here I am with a long Braille letter from Mr. Iwahashi entreating Polly and me to come to Japan. He wishes us to be there the middle of April.

Some time before Teacher's death this Mr. Takeo Iwahashi, champion of the blind in Japan, and blind himself, had called on Helen. After the first few minutes he understood her fairly well, but she had difficulty in reading his lips, so he resorted to Braille. He had come with an invitation.

"Will you come to Japan, Miss Keller, and open doors of help for our brothers and sisters shut out in great darkness, if I arrange with the Japanese government to sponsor the trip?"

Helen exclaimed that she could hardly believe her fingers. But she told him how impossible it was because of Teacher's illness. Mr. Iwahashi had bowed his understanding. "God's miracles never stop. Perhaps in a way higher than earth's ways he will help your teacher to see."

Early in December there had been a cable from the Japanese government begging her to come to Japan in the spring. Mr. Migel, head of the American Foundation for the Blind, wrote her an enthusiastic letter urging her to accept, and now she sat with Mr. Iwahashi's letter in her hand.

They sailed for home in February, and by the end of March were on their way to San Francisco. The Japanese hospitality began in the Grand Central Station in New York City when Helen felt tiny fingers trembling at her collar and smelled gardenia fragrance. "What is happening?" she wanted to know.

"A lady from the Japanese delegation here to send us off has given you a gardenia," replied Polly.

It was the beginning of a wonderful, exotic, and soul-challenging tour. Japan welcomed her more than royally; it welcomed her lovingly. Ambassador

Joseph Grew was there, and Takeo Iwahashi; there were government officials, and representatives of schools for the blind and the deaf. Her work began "with a rush which lifted my mind above personal suffering." There were conferences as to the best ways to educate and rehabilitate handicapped children; there were press conferences, as well as speeches and visits of inspection at the schools for the handicapped; and there was a garden party at the Imperial Palace where she and Polly were received by the emperor and empress.

They saw the cities and also quaint, out-of-the-way villages. They ate Japanese food, rather cautiously at first, in the Japanese fashion, squatting on their heels with as much grace as they could muster; and slept Japanese style on the floor. This was something which especially thrilled Helen, for as she lay on the *tatami* she could put her hand on the spotless matting and "watch" the vibrations of the sliding doors and windows, and the "pit-pat" of the feet as they passed. She felt close to everything and everybody in Japan. Every object was within easy reach of her hands—cups, fans, screens, the lovely silken *obis* of the girls and women; the heavenly loveliness of the blossoming cherry trees, the rocks and pools of the gardens, and the dwarf pines.

At Nara the priests invited her to climb a ladder to touch the feet of the Great Buddha: she was the first woman ever to have this sacred privilege. They let her grasp the rope and catch the vibrations of the mighty bell as it pealed out the glories of the Lord Buddha. She touched rice paddies and tea plants, and wherever she went she was thronged by loving crowds, not only the blind and the deaf, but everyone.

She toured Korea and also Manchuria. But of all the foreign countries she has ever visited, perhaps the place which is closest and dearest to her heart is Japan.

Ten years after her first visit she went back. Japan and her own country had been at grips in a savage war. Her country had dropped atomic bombs upon Japanese cities. This time she went at the request of the Commander of the American Occupation Forces, General Douglas MacArthur—and her welcome was even more stirring than on her first visit! The Japanese, particularly the women, feel a deep reverence for Helen. They filled the streets of Tokyo just to watch for her and gaze at her as she passed.

"For many generations, more than we can count," one of them told an American bystander, "we bow our heads and submit to blindness and beggery. This blind and deaf woman lifts her head high and teaches us to win our way by work and laughter. She brings light and hope to the heart. We Japanese women have need of that."

Sometimes Helen was sorely in need of it herself. When the Second World War held America in its hideous clutches Helen said it coiled itself around her heart "with burning anguish." She remembered the blinded and mutilated soldiers of the First World War only too well. How could *anyone* offer help? But when Nella Braddy suggested, "Why don't you go to the hospitals and find out directly what you can do for them? You have your two hands, your heart, and your faith," she and Polly braced themselves for the ordeal and sought permission.

For two and a half years they made the rounds of more than seventy hospitals. Helen forgot her crippled speech, her awkwardness in strange places. She only remembered her debt to these men. She worked at first only in the Army hospitals, but later she had permission to go into the Navy ones as well, and when she could distinguish between a sailor and a marine the men were delighted, although baffled, until Helen explained that really it was a simple matter—the marine's training had developed his arm and shoulder muscles; the sailor's arm was smooth.

She convinced them—and why not? She was living proof—that life was not finished because of blindness or deafness, or mutilation. She proved to them that even deprived of two senses, she could be very much alive to the pleasures of everyday life, and could take part in the routines of normal life. Perhaps she told them how much she enjoyed gardening, and how she weeded the borders of her own lawn herself, distinguishing the weeds from the flowers by touch. Perhaps she showed them how to tell white lilacs from purple ones by the difference in texture and perfume, accomplishments that would have sent her to the gallows in the days of witchcraft, but which were very encouraging to men who had suddenly lost either sight or hearing.

From the United States hospitals she and Polly were sent by the Foundation to investigate conditions of the blind in Europe. They visited the war-blinded in England, France, and Italy, and then a military plane took them from Naples to Athens to see conditions there. And it was while they were there that personal calamity struck. A cable that was handed them one afternoon reported briefly and starkly that their house had burned to the ground.

This was not the Forest Hills house. Too many sad memories had haunted that for both of them, and so after their return from Japan they had found a pretty little place in Westport, Connecticut, and called it "Arcan Ridge" after the home of Polly's brother in Scotland.

It was paralyzing to think of their little house, so crammed with its irreplaceable treasures—Teacher's letters, Mrs. Keller's, Mildred's, Mr. Hitz's, Dr. Bell's—all lost. Gone were Helen's priceless Braille library, the exquisite gifts from Japan, the mementoes from all over the world; and the most dreadful loss of all was the precious manuscript Helen had been working on off and on for the past twenty years, the book that was to be her last and finest,

Teacher. Helen moaned, and the sound stabbed Polly afresh.

"The Teacher book—and all my notes and data—" the words were like the cry of a stricken thing. "Polly, the thought of them is like a mutilation—" She stopped, and a slow red crept into her cheeks. "Oh, Polly, I am so ashamed, so ashamed to have said that, when I think of the little children we have seen here who have been both blinded and mutilated! This is not like parting from Teacher. I have you and Herbert left to me, and we are all sound and well."

"Yes, and we have you!" Polly flashed back.

They returned to Paris to meet Herbert Haas, who had been their general factotum for the past twelve years. He had sailed to Europe with them and gone to Holland to visit friends. One look at his stricken face told Polly that he, too, knew of their loss.

"I shouldn't have come," he kept repeating. "If I had stayed at home it might not have happened. And I promised Teacher I would take care of you both."

"If you had been home we might have lost you, too." Polly said, and Helen's hold on his hand tightened. "We have wonderful friends, you know, and some means. And millions of people in the world have neither."

But it was hard to comfort Herbert.

Returning to Westport was hard. It was on Christmas morning that the three of them walked over to what Helen described as "the grave of our precious home, where we stood spellbound by the ultimate blank."

Generous neighbors took them in. Arcan Ridge could be rebuilt and refurnished, and it was; even a new Braille library could be accumulated, but only Helen could rebuild the *Teacher* book—and she must do it from memory alone. Besides the three-quarters-finished manuscript, all her notes and letters that had been gathering for twenty years were gone.

Another author would surely have surrendered and turned away in utter despair. But not Annie Sullivan's pupil. Annie had taught Helen many things, but never the meaning of surrender. Now in Nella Braddy's home, on Nella's typewriter, she set to work again. The only favor she asked was to have the period key pointed out to her. Alone and in silence she worked, keeping her desk and her papers in strict order by herself, and always remembering the last word she had typed. She wrote as steadily as she could, although the work was often interrupted by her world travels in behalf of the blind and the deaf-blind, and her work at home for the American Foundation for the Blind, and not until the book was complete and was finally put into Braille, could she check her work. With all her various interruptions, it was ten years after the Arcan Ridge fire had destroyed her first manuscript that *Teacher* was published.

Helen intended it to be her final book. It is one of which Teacher herself would have been very proud. Not because it is about herself, but because with it Helen Keller took her place with the truly fine writers of any age, and proved that Charles Copeland had been a true prophet when he said she had it in her to write better than any other student, man or woman, whom he had ever taught.

Few teachers have been paid such a tribute.

Anne Sullivan Macy would have been humbly proud of *Teacher*, and the tribute that it is.

The
Perfect
Tribute

On November fifteenth, 1956, Helen and Polly made another journey. Compared with their world-circling trips, this one was a bare stone's throw from home. Helen was returning to the Perkins School for the Blind—not, however, to South Boston, the scene of her childhood sojourns, but to the spacious campus in Watertown that had been Perkins' home since 1912. She had come by special invitation, and for a very particular purpose.

As she crossed the wide entrance hall of the main building, someone guided her hands until they rested on the rounded surface of a familiar object. The lighting of her face betrayed her instant recognition. "It is the globe," she told Polly quickly. "The globe that has been the landmark for all Perkins children. It was almost the first thing Teacher showed me on my first visit to Perkins."

She stood still, memories crowding close about her; and it began to seem that the hall was filling with all the people who had made her days at Perkins so wonderful—bearded Mr. Anagnos, who had sent Teacher to her, and who had been so generous and loving until the "Frost King" episode; motherly Sophia Hopkins; Maria Moulton, the matron; Fanny Marrett, who had sacrificed her free time after school hours in order to satisfy a child's desire to learn French; Mary Riley, who had patiently tried to give her some perception of music; sturdy Edith Thomas and exquisitely beautiful Willie Elizabeth Robin, her companions in silence as well as blindness; her own protegé, Thomas Stringer—it seemed as though she must reach out and find them all. And how much Perkins had meant to her.

But it was none of this group her thoughts drew closest to her today. She was thinking most intently of Teacher. It was at Perkins that Teacher herself had studied, and when a little child's father had sent a desperate appeal for help to the director of Perkins it was to the twenty-year-old girl who had just graduated that Mr. Anagnos gave the challenge. And it was also here at Perkins, seventy years ago, that the girl had read herself sick, straining her poor eyes over Dr. Howe's reports, to make herself capable of bringing some sort of knowledge and happiness into a faraway little girl's vacant life.

Almost instinctively Helen reached out her hand. It was Polly Thomson who took it. Polly was dearer than anything else on earth to Helen now, but it suddenly seemed to her that for twenty years she had been filled with hungry longing for the touch of that other hand.

But she had not come to Perkins simply to remember her childhood. She was here to take part in two special events. First she was guest of honor at the "Helen Keller Luncheon," with famous educators of the deaf and blind present to do her honor. Then the company moved across the campus, and after a brief speech by Dr. Augustus Thorndike, president of the Perkins Corporation, Polly led Helen forward; and then with groping hands that suddenly trembled, Helen pulled a cord, unveiling a plaque set in the entranceway of Perkins' newest official building.

Very gently Polly drew Helen's fingers across the raised letters:

THE KELLER-MACY COTTAGE
DEDICATED TO
HELEN KELLER
AND
ANNE SULLIVAN MACY

For the three-fold purpose of
educating deaf-blind girls and boys,

277

training teachers of deaf-blind children,
performing research for the education of
deaf-blind youth

Slowly and with unusual distinctness, Helen repeated the words and dedicated the building, speaking of her own happiness in the project and the joy that would have been Teacher's to know of this work.

Riding home again, she and Polly sat with hands clasped in silent understanding. Helen was thinking of how greatly Teacher really would have rejoiced in the cottage that bore their names. She would delight in the pleasant, homelike atmosphere of the rooms, and believing as she did in surrounding all children, but especially handicapped ones, with beauty, she would have appreciated the charm of the place. She would have been glad that Perkins does not segregate these "children of the silent night"—that they live in other cottages, and come to this one just to be taught by their special teachers. Helen knew that Teacher's whole soul would have gone out to the director of Perkins' Deaf-Blind Department and his staff of teachers, attendants, and trainees, for the warm and deeply personal interest they take in their charges. Perhaps what would have pleased her most, Helen reflected, would be to know that the whole staff talks to these children exactly as though they were normal—following in the path she pioneered.

Anne Sullivan Macy had never been a schoolmarm, but there have been few people who were more fit to be called "Teacher."

As for Helen herself, of all the achievements she had learned about at Keller-Macy perhaps the one that thrilled her most was the progress in teaching by vibration. Now that a deaf-blind child is no longer tied to the finger language, but from the start of his education learns to catch words from another person's lips and to break the chains of his own silence, he can be taught to speak in a clear, intelligible and pleasing voice.

With all her fame, and the many honors and degrees bestowed upon her, there could never be a greater satisfaction than to know that, because she and Teacher had lived and struggled and triumphed as they did, and because of the work to be accomplished at the Keller-Macy Cottage at Perkins, other "children of the silent night" would live wider, brighter, easier lives than hers.

Helen Keller felt that nobody could receive a higher honor than the one that had been bestowed upon Teacher and upon her that day.

51461

AUG 27 1973	
SEP 5 1973	
SEP 6 1973	
SEP 7 1973	